SUCCESS WITH R

# SUCCESS WITH
# RICE

**INVADER**

# INTRODUCTION

## History

Rice has been a basic food for the majority of the world's population since ancient times. Archaeologists have found evidence that it was consumed by humans as long as 5000 years ago. Today, more than half the world's population regard rice as their staple diet.

The Chinese seem to have been the first people to grow rice as a food. From China, the cultivation of rice spread to other parts of Asia, reaching Indonesia, Malaysia, the Phillipines, India, Iran, and the coast of Africa. The ancient Greeks and the Romans included rice in their meals but it was not grown in Europe until the 11th century when the Moors introduced the cultivation of rice to Spain. From there, it spread to Italy and to South America.

In the 17th century, a ship loaded with rice was wrecked off the coast of Carolina in the United States. To repay the inhabitants who came to their aid, the captain of the ship made them a present of several sacks of rice. The fertile banks of the rivers in Carolina and Georgia proved ideal for growing rice and this was the beginning of rice cultivation in North America. 'Carolina Gold' rice has long been considered one of the best types of rice in the world.

Technological progress has since made American rice production one of the most efficient in the world. Mechanisation has allowed American farmers to cut production costs and reduce working time to just 14 hours per hectare (10,000 square metres). In some parts of Asia, it takes about 600 hours to cultivate one hectare.

## Cultivation of rice

The traditional image of rice growing on terraces or in paddy fields with hundreds of people bent over the plants, cultivating them by hand, is gradually changing, at least in the western world. In the United States, a laser is used to identify flat areas of land suitable for paddy fields. The fields are then separated by dykes (built by machine) which hold the water in. Rice seed is sown from aeroplanes and the fields are artificially flooded to allow the seeds to germinate. As soon as the rice is fully grown, the water is drained away so that tractors can move on to the fields to begin harvesting.

Harvesting can begin as soon as the grains of rice contain between 18 and 20 per cent of moisture. The untreated grains, the 'paddy', are then put into a drier to reduce the moisture level to about 12 per cent. This stage is necessary to prevent the rice from decaying. The rice is then steamed, peeled, polished, graded and wrapped mechanically. At no time does it need to pass through a worker's hands.

In 1613, a French Canadian settlement, at Port Royal in Nova Scotia, was destroyed by the British and many of the French settlers were deported to Louisiana in the southern United States. Here they founded a new Acadia, the capital of which was Lafayette. They depended for their survival on the marshy plains and rivers which covered the region. Their diet consisted of rice (the people of Louisiana eat almost as much rice as the Asians) accompanied by crayfish from the rivers. The descendants of these people, the Cajuns, still live in the region around Lafayette. The area is famous throughout the world for the delicious red crayfish which are so typical of traditional Cajun cooking. Cajun cuisine came about because the rice farmers discovered that the flooded paddy fields made an ideal habitat for crayfish.

# VARIETIES OF RICE

There are about 4000 different sorts of rice but only a few of these can be cultivated as food crops. The different varieties are classified in three groups: round-grain, medium-grain and long-grain rice.

The grains of round-grain, or short-grain, rice are 4-5 mm long and 2.5-3 mm wide, so they are almost as broad as they are long. They contain a large amount of starch and tend to stick together after cooking. This type of rice is generally used for puddings and is sometimes called 'dessert rice'.

The grains of medium-grain rice are a little longer but they are equally broad, measuring 5-6 mm in length and 2.5-3 mm in width. They contain an equally large amount of starch and also stick after cooking. Medium-grain rice may be used for puddings or in savoury dishes where the rice needs to be moulded or bound together.

The grains of long-grain rice are longer and more slender than the other two sorts. They are 6-8 mm long and about 1.5 mm wide. These grains contain a different sort of starch from the other types, thus they are suitable for dishes requiring firmer grains. The production of long-grain rice is limited and the largest producers are the United States, Thailand, Madagascar and some countries in South America.

European countries such as Spain and Italy cultivate a type of rice called Avorio. It has very large grains, containing a great deal of starch and it is particularly suitable for making risotto.

### Processing rice

An untreated grain of rice is composed of a hard outside husk, which may be round or oval, and a kernel which is surrounded by a layer of bran.

The many different sorts of rice that you can buy are distinguished by the particular milling process they have undergone. Wholegrain, or brown, rice undergoes the least refining. Only the outer husk is removed and the remaining grain is a light brown colour

8

1. WHITE, SHORT-GRAIN
2. BROWN, MEDIUM-GRAIN
3. WHITE, LONG-GRAIN
4. WHITE, MEDIUM-GRAIN
5. PARBOILED LONG-GRAIN
6. PRECOOKED, LONG-GRAIN

with a nutty taste. The bran, minerals and vitamins in the grain are all retained. Brown rice keeps for less time than other types, however. It needs a far longer cooking time than polished rice and requires more liquid. You can also buy a pre-cooked variety which cooks in a shorter time.

Wild rice is sometimes confused with brown rice but it is, in fact, the seeds of a wild grass. Wild rice is gathered in unpolluted lakeland regions of North America. It is harvested by hand, usually by Indian tribes who have been gathering this rice for centuries. Harvesting rice by hand is hard, demanding work which explains why this type of rice is expensive. It is often mixed with ordinary rice to keep the price down. Wild rice has a strong, distinctive flavour and smell. Nowadays, it is also cultivated in the United States. Cooking time is 45-50 minutes, as with brown rice, and the grains swell to four or five times their original volume. A little goes a long way!

White rice, or polished rice, is stripped of its outer husk and also the layer of bran. During this process, it loses the majority of its nutrients such as fats, fibre, minerals and vitamins, particularly those in the B group. Cooking time is reduced to 15 or 20 minutes. To compensate for the loss of vitamins and minerals, American rice is enriched with iron, niacin (one of the vitamin B group) and thiamine (vitamin B1). White rice keeps for an unlimited time.

The removal of the B group of vitamins from polished rice was the cause of an epidemic of beri-beri, a disease brought about by vitamin B deficiency. It is found in Asia but it has since spread elsewhere. This epidemic was only checked when a new method of processing rice was discovered in the United States. By steaming the rice grains under constant pressure, it is possible to retain 75 per cent of the vitamins and minerals contained in the grains. This type of rice, known as parboiled rice, should not be confused with steamed rice. Parboiled rice is harder, more compact and almost transparent. It does not stick after cooking and its nutritive value is greatly enhanced. It is not as nutritious as brown rice, therefore, but it does not lose nearly as much nutritive value as polished rice.

Precooked rice is polished, cooked and dried. The cooking time,

therefore, is reduced to a minimum. This type of rice is particularly convenient for quick meals or for puddings. The cooking instructions on the packet should be followed meticulously because these vary with different brands. Although most types of precooked rice are enriched with vitamins and minerals, their nutritive value is nevertheless reduced.

### Foreign varieties of rice

Rice can also be classifed under its country of origin. Indian rice (Basmati) has a slender, spicy grain. It is also cultivated in the United States and the spices are sometimes added artificially.

Japanese rice is a polished rice which contains a large amount of starch. Its quality is determined by how well the grains stick together. This is important to the Japanese who often eat rice with bread or with their hands. Chinese and Asian varieties are sticky for the same reason.

# COOKING METHODS

Cooking methods are given under the individual recipes. However, the following methods are some of the basic ways of preparing the different types of rice.

### The American method

This is the method most often used in western countries. It is not necessary to wash American rice. Mix 1 cup of long-grain rice with just over twice its volume of water. Add salt and a knob of butter. Quickly bring the water to the boil, without covering the pan. As soon as the water begins to boil, cover the pan and reduce the heat to a mininum. If you are using an electric cooker, turn it off altogether as enough heat will be retained in the hot-plate and its heat reduces gradually. Do not lift the lid. If, after 20 minutes, you do not think that the rice is dry enough, leave it to cook for a further 3-4 minutes.

Plain water can be replaced by vegetable juices, stock, a mixture of plain water and vegetable cooking water, or a mixture of water and white wine.

This method is particularly suitable for parboiled rice.

### Creole rice

Bring a large quantity of water to the boil with a little salt and add the rice. Bring back to the boil quickly and then reduce the heat. Simmer without a lid on the pan. The rice should be ready in 12-20 minutes, depending on the type you are using. Drain the cooked rice and rinse it in cold water. This method is less suitable for parboiled rice but is best for polished rice. It is not so easy to add extra flavouring such as saffron or vegetables when using this method, however, and some of the nutritive value is lost when you drain the rice.

### Pilaff rice (Turkish method)

First brown the rice in hot oil or butter, adding chopped vegetables, onion and garlic and stirring continuously. Then add 1-2 times the amount of water or stock, salt and pepper and bring to the boil. Cover and leave to cook over a very low heat, or on a turned-off electric ring, without lifting the lid. Check the rice after about 15 minutes.

### Risotto (Italian method)

This method is very similar to cooking pilaff, but the Italians use their own rice, Avorio. A good risotto should be thick and sticky. Heat some olive oil and brown a selection of chopped vegetables such as onion, garlic, mushrooms, tomatoes, pepper, courgettes or aubergines. Add the rice and brown quickly with the vegetables. Add some white wine or stock and simmer, stirring continuously. Add more liquid as necessary until the rice is cooked. Before serving, add a knob of butter and some grated Parmesan or Italian cheese.
Another method is to add all the liquid at once and simmer gently in a covered pan. The same method is used to make Spanish paella.

### Chinese steamed rice

Wash some Chinese rice (obtainable from Chinese shops) several times until the water is clear. Put the rice into a heavy pan with a little more than twice its volume of water. Bring to the boil and simmer for 15-20 minutes, until all the water has been absorbed. Remove the pan from the heat and cover. Slide a piece of kitchen towel between the lid and the pan. Leave rice to cook in the steam for 20 minutes.

### The Japanese method

Wash some Japanese rice (obtainable from Asian shops) several times until the water is clear. Drain and put into a pan. Fill with enough water to cover the rice with a centimetre of water and leave to soak for 30-60 minutes. Cover the pan and cook the rice gently for 10 minutes. Reduce the heat when the water begins to bubble and leave to simmer for about 4 minutes.

Reduce the heat to a minimum, or switch off if you are using an electric cooker, then leave to steam for 10 minutes, with the pan covered. Remove the lid and serve the rice with a dampened wooden spoon. Spoon the rice into individual bowls. Leave the rest of the rice in the pan with the lid wrapped in a towel. If you want to prepare Sushi rice, which should be cold and sticky, you should use a different method (see page 42).

### Rice cooked in a microwave

Cooking rice in a microwave oven is very easy; it also saves on energy and on washing up cooking pans. However, it takes just as long to cook rice in a microwave oven as it does on a conventional cooker. Always follow the cooking instructions given on the packet. If no instructions are given, use the following method.

For 1 cup of long-grain, brown or parboiled rice, add 1¾-2 cups, 2½-2 cups and 2-2½ cups of water respectively. Put rice and water into a microwave dish with a lid.
Cook long-grain rice for 5 minutes at maximum and 15 minutes at medium power; brown rice for 5 minutes at maximum and 45-55 minutes at medium; and parboiled rice for 5 minutes at maximum and 20 minutes at medium power.
These times are for a 700-watt oven.

### Levels of difficulty

This book contains some recipes which are quick and easy to prepare as well as others which are original and delicious, but need more work. The level of difficulty is indicated against each recipe as follows:
* = quick to prepare
** = requires more work
*** = for experienced cooks

AN IRRIGATED FIELD OF RICE IS CALLED A SAWA

2½ pints (1 litres) stock
  made from a cube
4½ oz (125 g) long-grain
  rice
1 leek
1 stick celery
½ cauliflower
4 small carrots
6 oz (150 g) fresh peas
2 oz (50 g) fresh chervil
pepper
salt

# SPRING SOUP*

*For four servings*

1  Add the rice to the stock and bring to the boil. Cover the pan and lower the heat until the stock is just boiling.
2  Meanwhile, wash the vegetables, cut the leek into thin circles, chop the celery and carrots into pieces and divide the cauliflower into florets. Shell the peas and chop the chervil.
3  When the rice has been simmering for 10 minutes, add the vegetables and leave to cool for 10 minutes, uncovered.
4  Put the chopped chervil into a bowl with a spoonful of stock and mix well.
5  Season the soup with salt and pepper and add the chervil mixture. Reheat without allowing to boil and serve immediately.

14 oz (400 g) pumpkin
  flesh
1 onion, finely chopped
2 cloves garlic, finely
  chopped
2¼ pints (1¼ litres)
  chicken stock
pepper
salt
nutmeg
3 oz (75 g) long-grain rice
7 fl oz (200 ml) water
4 oz (100 g) butter
2 slices white bread

# PUMPKIN SOUP WITH RICE*

*For four servings*

1  Cut the pumpkin flesh into cubes. Bring the stock to the boil, then cook the pumpkin, onion and garlic in it for 20 minutes. Season with salt, pepper and nutmeg.
2  Cook the rice in the water. Reduce the heat as soon as the water boils and simmer for 15 minutes, covered.
3  Put the pumpkin mixture into a blender and purée. Stir in the rice.
4  Cut the bread into small dice for croutons. Fry in half the butter, turning continuously.
5  Mix the rest of the butter into the soup while reheating and serve with the croutons.

# SOUPS AND STARTERS

PUMPKIN SOUP WITH RICE
SPRING SOUP

# FISH SOUP WITH RICE*

1 carrot
1 onion
1 stick celery
1 fillet of sole
1 fillet of turbot
1 oz (30 g) butter
1¾ pints (1 litre) water
16 fl oz (500 ml) dry
  white wine
salt
1 clove garlic, finely
  sliced
2 tbsps (2x15 ml spoons)
  cold pressed olive oil
7 oz (200 g) rice
1 lb 2 oz (500 g) sea
  bream fillets
2 oz (50 g) parsley

*For four servings*

1   Peel the carrot and the onion. Cut the onion into pieces. Wash the sole and turbot and brown gently in the butter. Chop parsley finely.
2   Add water, wine, onion, carrot and celery. Salt lightly and leave to cook for 30 minutes over a moderate heat.
3   In a separate pan, brown the garlic in the oil. Pour the strained vegetable liquid into the pan and add the rice.
4   Cut the fish fillets into small pieces and add them to the soup after about 15 minutes.
5   Cook for 5 minutes.
6   Mix chopped parsley into the soup.

# MUSSEL SOUP**

4 tbsps (4x15 ml spoons)
  olive oil
1 onion, finely chopped
2 cloves garlic, finely
  chopped
1 small stick celery, finely
  chopped
2¼ lb (1 kg) mussels,
  washed
freshly ground pepper
1 glass white wine
1¾ pints (1 litre) water
pinch curry powder
parsley, chopped
7 oz (200 g) rice

*For four servings*

1   Brown the onion and garlic in half the oil until transparent. Add half the celery and braise.
2   Add the mussels and season with pepper. Cover the pan and cook for 10 minutes until the mussels open. (Discard any mussels with shells that have not opened.)
3   Remove the mussels from their shells and strain the liquid from the mussels through muslin.
4   Brown the rest of the celery in the remaining olive oil. Add the mussel juice, white wine and water.
5   Bring to the boil, add the rice and cook for 15 minutes. Season with curry powder and reheat the mussels in the soup.
6   Sprinkle with parsley and serve immediately.

FISH SOUP WITH RICE
MUSSEL SOUP

RISOTTO WITH WILD MUSHROOMS AND COURGETTES
RISOTTO WITH SAFFRON AND PEAS

GENOESE RISOTTO
RISI-BISI

# RISOTTO

Risotto is a rice mixture made with vegetables and seasoned with butter and grated cheese.

## GENOESE RISOTTO**

*For four servings*

2 small onions, finely chopped
3 tbsps (3x15 ml spoons) olive oil
4 cups beef stock made from a cube
9 oz (250 g) Italian Avorio rice
1 can peeled tomatoes
8 fl oz (250 ml) tomato juice
fresh basil leaves, chopped
8½ oz (250 g) mushrooms, thinly sliced
pepper
salt
2 oz (50 g) Parmesan cheese, grated
1 oz (30 g) butter

1   Heat the oil in a large frying pan and lightly brown the onion.
2   Add unwashed rice and brown until grains become transparent. Drain the tomatoes and save 8 fl oz (250 ml) of the juice.
3   Cut the tomatoes in half. Add tomatoes and basil to the rice, and gradually add the stock and tomato juice while stirring continuously.
4   Cook the mushrooms in butter for 10-12 minutes.
5   When the rice is 'al dente', after 18-20 minutes, gently stir in the mushrooms. Season with pepper and salt, and add the Parmesan.

## RISOTTO WITH SAFFRON AND PEAS**

*For four servings*

4 oz (100 g) butter
1 onion, finely chopped
½ glass white wine
8½ oz (250 g) Avorio rice
a few saffron strands
1 small packet frozen peas
pepper
salt
2 oz (50 g) Parmesan cheese, grated
16 fl oz (500 ml) chicken stock

1   Put the onion and wine into a dish with half the butter. Cook uncovered in the microwave oven for 2 minutes on maximum power.
2   Add rice and saffron, and cook, uncovered, on maximum power for a further 2 minutes.
3   Add peas and stock, and season with pepper and salt.
4   Cover the dish and cook for 10 minutes on maximum power. Stir in the rest of the butter and sprinkle with Parmesan cheese.

8½ oz (250 g) wild
  mushrooms
2 tbsps (2x15 ml spoons)
  lemon juice
1 courgette
1 large onion
4 oz (100 g) butter
7 oz (200 g) Avorio rice
1¾ pints (1 litre) beef
  stock made from a cube
2 oz (50 g) Parmesan
  cheese, grated
3 tbsps (3x15 ml spoons)
  single cream
pepper
salt

# RISOTTO WITH WILD MUSHROOMS AND COURGETTES**

*For four servings*

1  Cut the mushrooms into pieces and sprinkle with lemon juice.
2  Wash the courgettes and cut into fine slices.
3  Peel the onion and chop finely.
4  Cook mushrooms in half the butter and season with pepper and salt. Remove from frying pan.
5  Brown the courgette and onion until transparent. Add the rice.
6  Gradually pour in the stock and stir from time to time.
7  Cook for about 18-20 minutes, making sure that the rice does not become too dry. Add the rest of the butter, the mushrooms, Parmesan cheese and cream. Stir in gently and serve immediately.

2 medium-sized onions
6 oz (150 g) streaky bacon
2-3 tbsps (2-3x15 ml
  spoons) olive oil or 1 oz
  (30 g) butter
5 cups beef stock made
  from a cube
1 lb (450 g) frozen peas
8½ oz (250 g) Avorio rice
pepper
salt
3 oz (75 g) Parmesan
  cheese, grated
¾ oz (20 g) butter

# RISI-BISI**

*For four servings*

1  Peel and chop the onions roughly. Dice the bacon.
2  Brown the onions and bacon in hot olive oil or butter.
3  Add 3 cups of stock and bring to the boil. Add peas and unwashed rice. Cook gently for 18-20 minutes, adding more stock from time to time.
4  Season with pepper and salt. At the end of the cooking time, add 1 oz (30 g) Parmesan and a knob of butter.
5  Serve the rest of the Parmesan cheese separately.

¾ oz (20 g) dried Chinese
   mushrooms
¾ oz (20 g) butter
7 oz (200 g)
   medium/round-grain
   rice
16 fl oz (500 ml) milk
pinch salt
6 oz (150 g) Parmesan
   cheese, grated
4 eggs, separated
breadcrumbs

# RICE SOUFFLÉ***

*For four servings*

1  Soak the mushrooms in lukewarm water, drain and cut into small pieces. Cook for 10 minutes in the butter.

2  Cook the rice in the milk with salt.

3  Add the cheese, egg yolks and mushrooms. Stir gently.

4  Grease an ovenproof dish with butter and sprinkle with breadcrumbs. Preheat the oven to 220°C/425°F or Gas Mark 7.

5  Beat the egg whites until stiff and fold into the rice mixture.

6  Pour the soufflé into the ovenproof dish and leave to rise in the oven for 30 minutes, without opening the door. Serve immediately.

1 onion, chopped
4 oz (100 g) butter
9 oz (250 g) rice
½ glass dry white wine
16 fl oz (500 ml) hot
   chicken stock made
   from a cube
pinch saffron
3 tbsps (3x15 ml spoons)
   Parmesan cheese, grated
8 eggs
pepper
salt
2 oz (50 g) ham, cut into
   small strips
2 oz (50 g) Gruyère
   cheese, grated
8 ramekins or small
   soufflé moulds

# RICE TARTLETS WITH BAKED EGGS**

*For eight servings*

1  Brown the onion in 1 oz (30 g) butter. Add the rice and wine. Mix thoroughly and gradually add the stock until the rice has absorbed all the liquid.

2  Mix saffron into the rice and, lastly, add the Parmesan cheese.

3  Preheat the oven to 200°C/400°F or Gas Mark 6. Plunge the ramekins into hot water, then butter them. Fill each ramekin with 2 tbsps (2x15 ml spoons) rice and crack an egg on top of each one.

4  Season with pepper and salt. Top with ham, Gruyère cheese and knobs of butter.

5  Put the ramekins into an ovenproof dish, fill to two-thirds with hot water and put into the oven for 6-8 minutes, until the egg whites are firm.

6  Serve with chilled white wine.

RICE TARTLETS WITH BAKED EGGS
RICE SOUFFLE

## TOMATOES STUFFED WITH RICE**

8 firm tomatoes
salt
3 tbsps (3x15 ml spoons)
   cold pressed olive oil
½ tsp (0.5x5 ml spoon)
   dried oregano
a sprig of fresh marjoram
a sprig of fresh mint,
   chopped
a sprig of fresh parsley
4 oz (100 g) medium/
   round-grain rice
8 fl oz (250 ml) chicken
   stock made from a cube
butter
freshly ground pepper

Stuffed tomatoes are a popular dish in Italy. The tomatoes are usually served cold but they can also be eaten hot.

*For four servings*

1   Cut the tops off the tomatoes and scoop out the insides. Sprinkle the tomatoes with salt and leave to drain in a sieve.
2   Chop the tomato flesh finely and mix with the rice. Stir in the herbs and olive oil.
3   Stir in the chicken stock. Pour the mixture into a microwave dish and cook uncovered for 10 minutes on maximum power.
4   Put the tomatoes into a greased microwave dish, fill each one with the rice mixture and cook uncovered for 10 minutes on maximum power.
5   Season with pepper and serve hot or cold.

## RICE CROQUETTES WITH SCAMPI TAILS**

1 oz (30 g) butter
9 oz (250 g) medium/
   round-grain rice
5 cups stock made from a
   cube
1 egg yolk
1 egg white, lightly beaten
pepper
salt
cayenne pepper
1 packet frozen scampi
   tails
breadcrumbs
oil for frying

*For four servings*

1   Heat the butter and brown the rice. Add stock and cook gently for 15 minutes.
2   Leave to cool. Add the egg yolk to the rice. Season with pepper, salt and cayenne pepper.
3   Shape the rice mixture into balls and put a scampi tail into each one, pressing the mixture firmly around it.
4   Roll the croquettes first in the egg white and then in the breadcrumbs.
5   Fry the croquettes in oil.

TOMATOES STUFFED WITH RICE
RICE CROQUETTES WITH SCAMPI TAILS

7 oz (200 g) long-grain
  rice
1 red pepper
2 spring onions
10 green olives
1 can artichoke hearts
2 tomatoes
2 tbsps (2x15 ml spoons)
  olive oil
3 tbsps (3x15 ml spoons)
  mayonnaise
pinch curry powder
freshly ground pepper
lemon juice

# RICE SALAD WITH PEPPERS AND ARTICHOKE HEARTS*

*For four servings*

1   Cook and drain the rice. Leave to cool.
2   Clean the pepper and onions. Cut the pepper into small pieces and slice the onions into rounds. Drain the olives and artichoke hearts. Cut the tomatoes into pieces.
3   Mix the rice with oil and add peppers, onion, olives and most of the artichoke hearts.
4   Stir the mayonnaise into the salad and season with curry powder and a little lemon juice. Garnish with pieces of tomato and artichoke heart.

7 oz (200 g) long-grain
  rice
1 tsp (1x5 ml spoon)
  mustard
2 tbsps (2x15 ml spoons)
  vinegar
pinch sugar
salt
freshly ground pepper
4 tbsps (4x15 ml spoons)
  oil
½ green pepper
½ yellow pepper
4 oz (100 g) green beans
4 oz (100 g) frozen peas
1 lettuce
2 apples, diced
bunch dill leaves, chopped

# RICE SALAD WITH VEGETABLES*

*For four servings*

1   Cook the rice in salted water.
2   Make a vinaigrette with mustard, vinegar, sugar, salt, pepper and oil. Mix the vinaigrette with the hot rice and leave to cool.
3   Cut the peppers and beans into small pieces.
4   Blanch the beans, peppers and peas for 2 minutes in lightly salted boiling water. Slice the heart of the lettuce into strips. Blanch the lettuce strips for a few seconds in hot water. Drain the vegetables in a sieve.
5   Mix the apple with the vegetables. Stir the vegetable mixture and most of the dill into the rice and leave to stand for several hours at room temperature. Garnish with the remaining dill.

# RICE SALADS

RICE SALAD WITH PEPPERS AND ARTICHOKE HEARTS
RICE SALAD WITH VEGETABLES

# WHOLEGRAIN RICE SALAD*

Wholegrain rice contains vitamins and minerals and is therefore more nutritious than other types. It is an important element of vegetarian cooking because it goes so well with all sorts of vegetables.

1 large cup wholegrain rice
2 cups water
1 tsp (1x5 ml spoon) turmeric
sea salt
2-3 tomatoes
½ cucumber, diced
1 onion, chopped
4 oz (100 g) tofu
3 tbsps (3x15 ml spoons) olive oil
2 tbsps (2x15 ml spoons) cider vinegar
pinch curry powder
freshly ground pepper

*For four servings*

1   Wash the rice until the water is clear. Put the rice into a pan, add the water, a little sea salt and turmeric, and cook gently for 1 hour. Leave to cool.
2   Cut the tomatoes into small pieces and divide the tofu into small cubes.
3   Make a vinaigrette with the oil, vinegar, pepper, salt and curry powder. Stir it into the rice.
4   Add the rest of the ingredients and serve with wholemeal bread.

# RICE SALAD WITH HERRINGS AND APPLE*

1 cup long-grain rice
2 cups water
4 herring fillets
2 Granny Smith apples, washed
juice of ¼ lemon
2 shallots
pepper
salt
4 tbsps (4x15 ml spoons) mayonnaise
3 tbsps (3x15 ml spoons) yoghurt
bunch fresh coriander, chopped

*For four servings*

1   Cook the rice in the water and leave to cool.
2   Skin the herring fillets and cut them into small pieces.
3   Cut each apple into quarters and remove the core. Cut quarters into small pieces and sprinkle with lemon juice. Peel the shallots and chop them finely.
4   Mix the yoghurt with mayonnaise and season with pepper and salt.
5   Mix all the ingredients together and sprinkle with coriander.

WHOLEGRAIN RICE SALAD
RICE SALAD WITH HERRINGS AND APPLE

1 can artichoke hearts
½ packet frozen peas and
  carrots
10 green olives
10 black olives
1 green pepper
1 yellow pepper
1 courgette
3 tbsps (3x15 ml spoons)
  olive oil
7 oz (200 g) long-grain
  rice, cooked
1 large onion
2 cloves garlic
4 cups chicken stock
½ small jar capers
1 small can tuna in
  vegetable oil
pepper
salt
chives

# ITALIAN RICE SALAD*

*For four servings*

1  Drain the artichoke hearts and cut them
   into pieces. Stone the olives and cut them
   into strips. Defrost the peas and carrots.
2  Cut the carrots into pieces. Chop the
   peppers and courgette into small pieces.
   Peel and chop onion and garlic cloves
   finely. Drain and flake the tuna.
3  In a paella pan or a flat frying pan, brown
   the onion and garlic quickly in very hot
   oil. Add the vegetables, olives and cold
   rice and mix well.
4  Gradually pour the stock into the pan and
   braise gently.
5  When cooked, add the capers with their
   juice and the tuna.
6  Put the rice into a dish and leave in the
   refrigerator to chill.
7  Decorate with chives and serve cold.

7 oz (200 g) rice
salt
2 papayas
1 green pepper
1 can sweetcorn, drained
1 can tuna
6 tbsps (6x15 ml spoons)
  olive oil
2 tbsps (2x15 ml spoons)
  lime juice
pepper
cayenne pepper
bunch chives, finely
  chopped

# EXOTIC RICE SALAD*

*For four servings*

1  Cook the rice for about 20 minutes in
   salted water.
2  Remove the rice from heat and leave
   to cool.
3  Peel the papayas, remove the seeds and
   cut the flesh into small pieces. Cut the
   pepper into thin strips. Drain and flake
   the tuna.
4  Make a vinaigrette by mixing the lime
   juice, pinch of salt, oil, pepper, cayenne
   pepper and chives.
5  Mix all the ingredients into the cold rice
   and serve with fresh rolls or baguette.

ITALIAN RICE SALAD
EXOTIC RICE SALAD

# JAMBALAYA**

The cuisine of the southern United States, particularly Louisiana, is essentially French cooking with a marked Spanish and African influence, which also gave rise to Creole cuisine.

The Cajuns and the Creoles have enlivened American cooking with hot, spicy dishes such as jambalaya, crayfish pie, bouillabaisse, court-bouillon and gumbo.

8 shallots
1 small Spanish chilli
4 cloves garlic
9 oz (250 g) ham, in one piece
9 oz (250 g) chicken fillet
7 oz (200 g) butter
3 tbsps (3x15 ml spoons) flour
1 can peeled tomatoes
2 bay leaves
pinch cumin grains
3 cloves
8 Jamaican peppercorns
pinch cayenne pepper
10 black peppercorns
3 cups beef stock made from a cube
2 cups American long-grain rice
salt
1 packet frozen scampi tails
2 small onions

*For 8-10 servings*

1   Peel the shallots and the garlic cloves and chop them. Slice the Spanish chilli into rings.
2   Dice the ham and chicken. Cook them in the butter in a heavy frying pan.
3   Add shallots, garlic and chilli, and fry for 3 minutes.
4   Add flour and mix until lightly browned. Add the tomatoes with their juice and the bay leaves. Continue cooking on a lower heat.
5   Pound the spices to a coarse powder with a pestle and mortar. Add to the pan. Mix in well.
6   Add the stock and rice, season with salt and stir. Cover and simmer for 15 minutes.
7   Drop the frozen scampi tails onto the rice and cook in the steam for about 5 minutes.
8   Put the jambalaya into a large dish, garnish with small onions.
9   Heat jambalaya in the oven for a few minutes. Serve very hot.

# RICE WITH FISH AND SHELLFISH

JAMBALAYA

# GUMBO WITH PRAWNS**

Gumbo is an old Creole dish which can include almost anything: deep-sea prawns, oysters, crab, turkey, and even alligator! Like jambalaya, it is a very spicy dish.

The classic Creole speciality is made with ground sassafras leaves. You will probably have some difficulty in finding these, however, but another way to make authentic gumbo is to replace the sassafras powder with okra, or 'ladies' fingers', which is available from most supermarkets.

The base of this dish is always a roux made from oil, or butter, and flour. The rice is cooked until it is quite dry, then it is poured on the gumbo.

2 tbsps (2x15 ml spoons) oil
1 tbsp (1x15 ml spoon) flour
3 tbsps (3x15 ml spoons) butter
2 onions
1 green pepper
1 small can peeled tomatoes
2 cloves garlic
pepper
salt
thyme
bay leaves
cayenne pepper
16 fl oz (500 ml) chicken stock (from a cube)
1 lb 2 oz (500 g) deep-sea prawns (or scampi tails)
7 oz (200 g) long-grain rice
2 spring onions

*For four servings*

1   Beat the oil and flour together in a saucepan and simmer, stirring continuously.
2   Chop the onion roughly and fry the pieces in butter for 5 minutes.
3   Crush the garlic cloves. Cut the pepper into small pieces and add to the onion. Stir in the tomatoes and garlic. Leave to simmer for 20 minutes.
4   Season with pepper, salt, thyme, bay leaves and cayenne pepper.
5   Pour in the stock and cook for another 20 minutes.
6   Meanwhile, cook the rice.
7   Add the prawns to the sauce and cook for 5 minutes.
8   Drain the rice and serve on a plate garnished with the chopped green leaves of spring onions.

GUMBO WITH PRAWNS

6 oz (150 g) broad beans
1 lb 2 oz (500 g) calamari
salt
1 onion
2 oz (60 g) butter
14 oz (400 g) Italian
   risotto rice
7 fl oz (200 ml) dry white
   wine
1¾ pints (1 litre) chicken
   stock made from a cube
bunch parsley, chopped

# RISOTTO WITH CALAMARI AND BEANS**

*For four servings*
1   Soak the beans in water overnight.
2   Cook beans for 1 hour 15 minutes and then drain well.
3   Rinse the calamari in cold water and cook for 40 minutes in salted water. Rinse them in cold water and remove the outer skin. Cut flesh into small pieces.
4   Chop the onion finely and fry in half the butter.
5   Add the rice and cook for 1 minute, stirring gently. Add wine and allow to evaporate. Gradually pour in the stock.
6   After 9 minutes, add the beans and calamari, and cook for a further 9 minutes. Add the rest of the butter with the chopped parsley. Remove the pan from the heat and continue to stir for another 2 minutes.
7   Season with pepper and salt.

10½ oz (300 g) calamari,
   with the ink sacs
1 clove garlic
1 shallot
3 tbsps (3x15 ml spoons)
   olive oil
pepper
salt
14 oz (400 g) Italian
   risotto rice
1¾ pints (1 litre) stock
   made from a cube
2 oz (60 g) butter
bunch parsley, chopped

# BLACK RISOTTO***

*For four servings*
1   Clean the calamari and then soak in cold water. Remove the skin and cut the flesh into pieces.
2   Peel and chop the garlic and shallot finely. Fry them in olive oil until transparent.
3   Add the calamari pieces and braise for 30 minutes.
4   Add the rice mixed with stock, then add the calamari ink and mix thoroughly. Leave to simmer for 15 minutes.
5   Add the butter and chopped parsley. Season with pepper and salt.

BLACK RISOTTO
RISOTTO WITH CALAMARI AND BEANS

1 roasting chicken and 2
  chicken legs
pepper
salt
1 tsp (1x5 ml spoon)
  mixed herbs
4 tbsps (4x15 ml spoons)
  olive oil
1 lb 2 oz (500 g) calamari
10½ oz (300 g) mussels
1 large onion
1 red pepper
1 green pepper
4 tomatoes
3 chorizo sausages
2 tbsps (2x15 ml spoons)
  olive oil
1 clove garlic, crushed
1 lb 2 oz (500 g) round-
  grain rice
pinch saffron
1¾ pints (1 litre) stock
  made from a cube
salt
6 oz (150 g) frozen peas
10½ oz (300 g) frozen
  king prawns or deep-sea
  prawns
9 oz (250 g) scampi tails
9 oz (250 g) cockles

# PAELLA VALENCIANA**

*For 6-8 servings*

1 Wash the chicken and chicken legs and
  dry carefully with kitchen paper. Divide
  into 12-16 portions, sprinkle with salt,
  pepper and herbs. Brown chicken pieces
  in olive oil until golden. Remove from
  the frying pan and set aside.
2 Defrost the calamari, wash and cut into
  rings.
3 Make sure that all the mussels are
  completely closed. Remove any with
  open shells and wash the others.
4 Chop the onion roughly. Wash the
  peppers and cut into strips. Brown the
  onion and peppers until transparent, using
  the oil left over from frying the chicken.
5 Plunge the tomatoes into boiling water
  for about 10 seconds then peel them,
  remove the seeds and chop the flesh. Add
  to the onions and peppers and cook
  gently.
6 Slice the sausages into rounds and add to
  the mixture.
7 Put the sausage and vegetable mixture
  into a large paella pan or a roasting tin.
8 Heat 2 tbsps (2x15 ml spoons) of olive oil
  in a pan and then add the rice and garlic,
  and cook until transparent.
9 Add the saffron and pour in the stock.
  Cook for 5 minutes and then add to the
  vegetables.
10 Put the chicken pieces, prawns, calamari,
   mussels and cockles on to the rice and
   then add the frozen peas on top. Season
   with salt and cook in a preheated oven at
   200°C/400°F or Gas Mark 6 for 25-30
   minutes.
11 Serve with red wine and crusty white
   bread.

PAELLA VALENCIANA

# JAPANESE SUSHI RICE***

When preparing sushi, it is essential that the rice sticks together in small parcels. Sushi is rice flavoured with vinegar and sugar. It is seasoned with wasabi (a paste made from Japanese horseradish) and served lukewarm, garnished with strips of raw fish and seaweed. Fish used for garnishing sushi should be very fresh. Salmon, tuna or calamari are all excellent. You can also decorate the sushi parcels with salmon's eggs, trout's eggs or even caviar. If you do not care for raw fish, you can replace it with smoked salmon, halibut or trout.

3 cups Japanese rice
  (short, round grains)
1 slice kombu (dried
  seaweed)
2 tbsps (2x15 ml spoons)
  rice wine or dry white
  wine
5 tbsps (5x15 ml spoons)
  rice vinegar or cider
  vinegar
2 tbsps (2x15 ml spoons)
  sugar
2 tsps (2x5 ml spoons) salt

*Garnish:*
fresh raw or smoked fish
  (salmon, tuna, calamari)
trout's or salmon's eggs
wasabi (green horseradish
  paste)
soy sauce
nori (dried seaweed
  leaves)

*For eight servings*

1   Rinse the rice three or four times until the water is clear. Drain in a sieve and leave to swell for 1 hour.
2   Cut kombu into pieces.
3   Mix the rice with wine, kombu and just over 3 cups of water in a large saucepan. Cook over a good heat.
4   Remove the kombu, lower the heat and cook for 10 minutes with a towel between the lid and the pan.
5   Mix sugar and salt into the vinegar. Put the rice into a large dish and add the mixture. Mix quickly with a wooden spoon and leave to cool.
6   Cover with a damp cloth.
7   Each guest is given a portion of rice which is the size of a mouthful. Smear each of these mouthfuls with a little wasabi and put some fish eggs or a strip of raw fish on top.
8   Tie the rice parcels with strips of nori and dip them in soy sauce.

JAPANESE SUSHI RICE

4½ lb (2 kg) mussels
5 onions
freshly milled pepper
3 tbsps (3x15 ml spoons)
  olive oil
9 oz (250 g) long-grain
  rice
7 fl oz (200 ml) dry white
  wine
1 red pepper, diced
1 green pepper, diced
1¾ lb (800 g) scampi tails

# GREEK PILAFF WITH MUSSELS**

*For six servings*

1  Clean the mussels and discard any that have opened.
2  Roughly chop one onion and put it into a large saucepan with the mussels. Season well with pepper and cook over a good heat until the mussels shells open. Shake the pan from time to time.
3  Discard any mussels that have not opened. Remove the shells from the others and strain the cooking liquid into a container.
4  Chop the remaining onions finely and brown in olive oil. Add the rice and mix thoroughly.
5  Add the juice from the mussels and the wine, and cook uncovered gently for 15-18 minutes.
6  Add the peppers and cook for 5 minutes.
7  Add the scampi tails and cook for 5 minutes. Garnish with mussels.

1 large onion
2 cloves garlic
1 carrot
3 tbsps (3x15 ml spoons)
  olive oil
1 lb 6 oz (600 g) scampi
6 oz (150 g) long-grain
  rice
1 tbsp (1x15 ml spoon)
  tomato purée
8 fl oz (250 ml) white
  wine
fish stock made from a
  cube
pepper
salt
3 oz (75 g) mature goat's
  cheese, cut into pieces
bunch fresh coriander,
  finely chopped

# TURKISH PILAFF WITH SCAMPI**

*For four servings*

1  Peel the onion and garlic. Chop finely. Wash and dice the carrot.
2  Glaze the vegetables in olive oil. Add the rice and tomato purée.
3  Add the wine and enough fish stock to thin the sauce.
4  Cook gently with the pan covered for 20-25 minutes.
5  Cook the scampi tails in water. Drain and peel them. Add scampi to the rice pilaff and season with salt and pepper. Reheat for a short while.
6  Sprinkle with the goat's cheese and coriander.

TURKISH PILAFF WITH SCAMPI
GREEK PILAFF WITH MUSSELS

45

# EXOTIC RICE WITH CHICKEN*

Rice and chicken are an excellent combination. In fact, any sort of poultry goes well with rice when it is served with vegetables or fruit. Fruit in particular adds an exotic flavour and appearance to this kind of dish. The exotic effect can be enhanced by using spices such as cardamom, paprika, saffron, chilli or curry powder, or sauces such as soya, chilli or oyster sauce. Beware of adding too many spices, however. The combination of too many flavours may give a disappointing result. Stick to a specific ingredient that will give your dish a dominant flavour. The recipe below involves using curry powder, but this can be replaced with cardamom, for example.

1 lb 10 oz (750 g) chicken breast
salt
3 tbsps (3x15 ml spoons) soy sauce
3 tbsps (3x15 ml spoons) mild curry powder
2 onions
2 cooking apples
3 oz (80 g) butter or margarine
10 oz (300 g) long-grain rice
2 oz (50 g) grapes
chicken stock made from a cube
1 star fruit
7 oz (200 g) fresh baby sweetcorn
7 oz (200 g) king prawns
2 spring onions, chopped
1 oz (30 g) flaked almonds

*For six servings*

1   Cut the meat into strips, season lightly with salt and mix in soy sauce.
2   Peel the onions and chop roughly. Peel and core the apples and dice the flesh.
3   Mix onion and apple together in a saucepan, add curry powder and half the butter or margarine. Add the rice and grapes, pour on the stock and bring to the boil. Cover the pan and simmer for 20 minutes.
4   Slice the star fruit and cook in a separate pan with the sweetcorn, using the rest of the fat. Remove from the pan. Cook the meat in the pan.
5   Put all the ingredients into a large paella pan. Sprinkle the prawns on top and cook in the preheated oven at 200°C/400°F or Gas Mark 6 for 10 minutes.
6   Just before serving, sprinkle with spring onions and flaked almonds.

# RICE WITH POULTRY

EXOTIC RICE WITH CHICKEN

4 chicken legs
  (1¾ lb/800 g)
pepper
salt
paprika powder
1 lb 2 oz (500 g)
  aubergines
1 lb 2 oz (500 g) tomatoes
3 oz (75 g) lean bacon
1 or 2 cloves garlic,
  crushed
4½ fl oz (125 ml)
  vegetable stock
sprigs of thyme, chopped
9 oz (250 g) long-grain
  rice

# RICE WITH CHICKEN LEGS AND AUBERGINES*

*For four servings*

1   Wash the chicken legs and dry carefully. Sprinkle with pepper, salt and paprika.
2   Wash the tomatoes and aubergines. Cut aubergines in two lengthways and slice. Plunge the tomatoes into boiling water for 10 seconds. Peel them and divide into eight pieces. Remove the seeds.
3   Cut the bacon into thin strips and brown in a frying pan.
4   Put the chicken legs into the bacon fat, sprinkle garlic on top and add the aubergines. Add the vegetable stock and simmer for 35-40 minutes.
5   Meanwhile, cook the rice in lightly salted water.
6   Add the tomatoes to the chicken 20 minutes before the end of the above cooking time.
7   Sprinkle with thyme.

1 small roasting chicken
paprika powder
bay leaves, chopped
1 cup basmati rice
4 tbsps (4x15 ml spoons)
  frozen peas
handful of cherry
  tomatoes
salt
freshly ground pepper

# SPIT-ROASTED CHICKEN WITH RICE AND VEGETABLES*

*For two servings*

1   Season the chicken with paprika and bay leaves, put on a spit and cook for 1 hour at 180°C/350°F or Gas Mark 4.
2   Wash the rice several times until the water is clear. Put it into a saucepan with 2 cups of water. Add peas and tomatoes, and season with salt and pepper.
3   Bring to the boil, cover and turn off the heat. Steam for 20 minutes without lifting the lid. Serve with the chicken and a green salad.

SPIT ROASTED CHICKEN WITH RICE AND VEGETABLES
RICE WITH CHICKEN LEGS AND AUBERGINES

RICE WITH CHICKEN AND LIME

CHICKEN LIVERS WITH GLAZED LEEKS

# RICE WITH CHICKEN AND LIME*

The Chinese cook rice by steaming it. The heat is turned off and the rice continues to cook in the steam, in a tightly sealed pan.

1 chicken breast
1 red pepper
9 oz (250 g) mushrooms
1 clove garlic
1 piece fresh root ginger
1 lime
1 cup flour
pepper
salt
2 oz (60 g) margarine
1 glass white wine
2 cups Chinese rice (long grain)

*For four servings*

1 Chop the chicken breast into small pieces. Clean the pepper, remove the seeds and cut into small pieces.
2 Peel the mushrooms and garlic. Chop the garlic clove finely. Peel the ginger, cut it into fine strips and then into *julienne.*
3 Remove the zest from the lime and squeeze half the juice.
4 Toss the chicken in the flour and season with salt and pepper.
5 Wash the rice several times until the water is clear. Put rice into a heavy saucepan and add a little more than twice its volume of water. Bring to the boil and cook, uncovered, until the water has been absorbed.
6 Remove the pan from the heat and place a towel between the lid and the pan. Cook rice in the steam for 20 minutes.
7 Heat a wok over a good heat, melt half the margarine and cook the chicken in it, turning all the time.
8 After 3 minutes, remove the chicken and drain.
9 Melt the rest of the margarine and cook the mushrooms and pepper.
10 Add the garlic, ginger, lime juice and wine. Cook for 2 minutes, stirring constantly.
11 Add the chicken and simmer for 3 minutes.
12 Garnish with lime zest and serve with steamed rice.

# CHICKEN LIVERS WITH GLAZED LEEKS **

In this recipe, two methods of Chinese preparation are used successively; shao and chao. 'Shao' involves leaving the ingredients to simmer, uncovered, on a low heat. The pieces of leek are cooked in this manner together with the vinegar, sugar and herbs until all the water has been absorbed. This results in a thick sauce and a glazing on the leeks. The second method, 'chao' is stir-frying in a wok. The wok is heated before the oil is poured in and the vegetables are stirred thoroughly while they cook.

*For four servings*

4 leeks
2 shallots
14 oz (400 g) chicken livers
2 oz (50 g) butter
2 tbsps (2x15ml spoons) oil
2 tsps (2x5 ml spoons) sugar
pinch cumin
pepper
salt
1 tsp (1x5 ml spoon) vinegar
bunch chives, chopped
2 cups Chinese rice

1  Wash the rice several times until the water is clear. Put the rice into a heavy pan with just over double its volume of water. Bring to the boil and cook for 15-20 minutes, uncovered, until all the water has evaporated.

2  Remove the pan from the heat and put a towel between the lid and the pan. Steam the rice for 20 minutes.

3  Clean the leeks and cut into pieces. Peel the shallots and chop roughly. Trim the chicken livers.

4  Heat the wok over a medium heat, melt half the butter and oil, add the leeks, sprinkle with sugar, cumin, pepper and salt, and add the vinegar. Cook for 4 minutes, stirring from time to time.

5  Remove the leeks from the wok and drain them on kitchen paper. Heat the oil, together with the rest of the butter, over a good heat. Brown the livers for 2 minutes, stirring constantly.

6  Add the leeks and cook for 1 more minute. Divide the liver mixture and the rice into separate Chinese bowls, and garnish with chopped chives.

3 cups chicken stock
1 onion
1 clove garlic
1 piece root ginger
black peppercorns
2 cardamom seeds
½ tsp (0.5x5 ml spoon)
  cumin seeds
a few coriander seeds
½ tsp (0.5x5 ml spoon)
  ground fennel
1 stick cinnamon
bay leaves
3 tbsps (3x15 ml spoons)
  oil
2 spring onions
1½ cups basmati rice
salt

# INDIAN RICE WITH CHICKEN CURRY**

*For four servings*

1   Bring chicken stock to the boil.
2   Peel the onion, garlic and ginger. Chop finely. Mix onion, garlic, ginger and spices into the stock. Leave for about 30 minutes for stock to absorb the flavours, then strain.
3   Chop the spring onions. Heat the oil in a saucepan and brown the spring onions. Add the rice and cook, stirring continuously.
4   Pour the strained stock on to the rice and simmer gently for 35 minutes, with a lid on the saucepan.

1 onion
1 clove garlic
1 lb 2 oz (500 g) chicken
  breast
2 tsps (2x5 ml spoons)
  vegetable oil
1 tsp (1x5ml spoon)
  turmeric
½ tsp (0.5x5 ml spoon)
  ground coriander
1 tsp (1x5 ml spoon) chilli
  powder
1 tsp (1x5 ml spoon)
  tomato purée
8 fl oz (250 ml) chicken
  stock (from a cube)
2 oz (50 g) grated coconut
2 oz (50 g) dried prunes
pepper
salt
9 oz (250 g) cooking
  apples
1 banana
basmati rice

# CHICKEN CURRY*

*For four servings*

1   Peel the onion and garlic. Chop them very finely. Dice the chicken.
2   Cook chicken and onion in very hot oil for 6 minutes, turning all the time. A wok can be used for this.
3   Add turmeric, coriander, cumin, chilli powder and garlic, and simmer for 5 minutes.
4   Add tomato purée, stock, coconut and prunes, and season with salt and pepper.
5   Cover the pan and reduce the heat. Simmer for 45 minutes.
6   Wash the apples, peel and dice them. Slice the banana into circles.
7   Add the fruit to the curry and simmer for a further 10 minutes. Serve with basmati rice.

INDIAN RICE WITH CHICKEN CURRY
CHICKEN CURRY

55

# RICE WITH CHICKEN IN SAUCE DIABLE*

Using a microwave oven does not necessarily save time when cooking rice because different types take different times and require different amounts of water. Traditional cooking methods are best for rice. Having cooked the rice in the conventional way, however, the accompanying ingredients can be prepared in the microwave oven. The cooked rice may be reheated in the microwave oven.

9 oz (250 g) long-grain rice
1 roasting chicken
pepper
salt
cayenne pepper
2 oz (50 g) butter or margarine
6 oz (150 g) mushrooms
1 can peeled tomatoes
4 fl oz (100 ml) chicken stock
handful parsley, chopped

*For four servings*

1 Put the rice in a saucepan with 2 times its volume of water. Bring to the boil without covering the pan.
2 Cover the pan as soon as the water is bubbling. Lower heat and cook rice for about 20 minutes or until it is dry.
3 Clean and cut chicken into 8 pieces. Season them with pepper, salt and a little cayenne pepper.
4 Heat the butter or margarine and brown the chicken pieces on all sides.
5 Put the mushrooms and tomatoes into a microwave dish and lay the chicken pieces on top.
6 Pour stock on to the chicken, making sure it is well coated.
7 Cover and cook in the microwave oven for 10 minutes at maximum power.
8 Remove the chicken pieces and cook the sauce for 1 more minute on maximum power, uncovered.
9 Pour the sauce on to the chicken and sprinkle with parsley.
10 Serve with rice.

RICE WITH CHICKEN IN SAUCE DIABLE

# IRANIAN PILAFF WITH CHICKEN*

In eastern cooking, rice is often combined with almonds or walnuts, or with grapes or other types of fresh or dried fruit. Saffron or turmeric are added to give the rice a rich, yellow colour.

2 chicken breasts (about 1 lb 6 oz/600 g)
salt
14 oz (400 g) carrots
2 oz (60 g) butter
1 oz (30 g) crystallized orange peel, finely chopped
14 oz (400 g) rice
4 oz (100 g) flaked almonds
a few saffron strands

*For six servings*

1   Remove skin from the chicken breasts and put them into a saucepan. Just cover with lightly salted water. Cook for 10 minutes then remove from heat and leave to cool in the cooking water.
2   Clean carrots and slice into thin circles. Cook carrots in lightly salted water until tender, then drain.
3   Melt half the butter in a small pan, cook the carrots in it for 5 minutes. Add the orange peel and cook for a further 5 minutes on medium heat.
4   Cook the rice for 5 minutes in 3 pints (2 litres) salted water. Drain.
5   On a low heat, brown the flaked almonds in ¼ oz (10 g) butter. Remove chicken from the water and chop into small pieces.
6   Melt the rest of the butter in a large frying pan, add half the rice and sprinkle a cup of water over it.
7   Add half the chicken pieces, almonds and carrots. Spread half the rest of the rice on top and add another layer of chicken, almonds and carrots. Cover with the rest of the rice.
8   Mix the saffron with ½ pint (300 ml) water and pour over the mixture.
9   Cover the pan and cook gently for 15 minutes.

IRANIAN PILAFF WITH CHICKEN

# RICE WITH BREAST OF DUCK AND GINGER**

In eastern cooking, rice is often steamed. As soon as the water boils, the heat is turned off and the rice is cooked for 20 minutes in a covered saucepan.

2 oz (50 g) fresh root
  ginger
juice of 1 lime
2 tsps (2x5 ml spoons)
  cane sugar
2 tbsps (2x15 ml spoons)
  white rum
freshly ground green
  peppercorns
salt
2¼ lb (1 kg) breast of duck
9 oz (250 g) Chinese rice
  (long grain)
1 can (500 g) pineapple
  slices, unsweetened
2 kiwi fruit
20 cherry tomatoes

*For four servings*

1   Peel the ginger and chop finely. Marinate the breast of duck in the ginger, lime juice, sugar, rum, pepper and salt for 2 hours.

2   Drain and save the marinade. Dry duck thoroughly. Put in a frying pan, skin side down, and brown without adding fat. Alternatively, brown on a barbecue with the grill about 5 inches (12 cm) above the charcoal.

3   Cook for 15 minutes, turn and cook the other side for 5 minutes.

4   Wash the rice several times until the water is clear. Put into a heavy saucepan with a little over twice its volume of water. Bring to the boil and cook for 15-20 minutes, uncovered, until the water has been completely absorbed.

5   Remove the pan from the heat and cover with a lid wrapped in a towel. Steam for 20 minutes.

6   Cut pineapple slices in two. Gently heat the marinade for 10 minutes, add the pineapple and cook for a further 5 minutes.

7   Peel and slice the kiwi fruit. Wash the cherry tomatoes.

8   Arrange the duck on plates with slices of kiwi fruit, pineapple pieces in sauce, and cherry tomatoes.

9   Add the rice and serve.

RICE WITH BREAST OF DUCK AND GINGER

# BALKAN GUINEA FOWL WITH RICE**

Like many other rice-based dishes, Balkan guinea fowl tastes better on the following day. You can of course reheat the dish in the microwave oven.

1 guinea fowl
6 oz (150 g) lean bacon
4 oz (100 g) onions
½ tsp (0.5x5 ml spoon)
  paprika powder
pepper
salt
1 lb 2 oz (500 g) green
  pepper
10 oz (300 g) ripe
  tomatoes
10 oz (300 g) long-grain
  rice
4 tsps (4x5 ml spoons)
  olive oil
bunch parsley, chopped

*For four servings*

1   Clean the guinea fowl and cut into pieces. Begin by cutting off the legs and the wings. Then cut the carcass in half lengthways. Cut the halves into two. Peel and chop onions.

2   Dice the bacon and brown it in a frying pan.

3   Remove bacon from pan and brown onion in bacon fat. Stir in paprika and add a little water.

4   Arrange the pieces of guinea fowl in the pan, with the liver on top, season with pepper and salt. Cover the pan and cook gently for about 30 minutes, turning from time to time.

5   Remove the seeds from the peppers and chop the flesh. Cut the tomatoes into pieces.

6   Wash the rice several times until water is clear, then drain in a sieve.

7   Heat the olive oil in a separate pan and cook the rice for a few minutes. Add the meat, peppers and tomatoes, and 21 fl oz (600 ml) water.

8   Cover the pan and simmer for 20-25 minutes.

9   Arrange the rice mixture on plates and sprinkle with parsley.

BALKAN GUINEA FOWL WITH RICE

1 grapefruit
9 oz (250 g) basmati rice
6 oz (150 g) butter
handful grapes
1 lb 6 oz (600 g) turkey
  breast
1 pepper
olive oil
dried thyme
cumin seeds
pepper
salt
½ tsp (0.5 x 5 ml spoon)
  turmeric
1 tsp (1x5 ml spoon)
  honey

# INDIAN RICE WITH TURKEY KEBABS**

*For four servings*

1  Peel the grapefruit like an apple, removing all the pith and the core. Cut the flesh into quarters.
2  Cook the rice in half the butter and add about 14 fl oz (400 ml) water. Add the grapefruit quarters and grapes. Cover the pan and cook gently for 20 minutes.
3  Put pieces of turkey and pepper on to skewers, coat with olive oil and grill for 15 minutes under a hot grill, turning from time time.
4  Season with thyme, cumin, pepper and salt.
5  Mix turmeric and honey into the rice with the rest of the butter.

7 oz (200 g) turkey fillet
2 carrots
½ yellow pepper
½ green pepper
1 onion
1 clove garlic
1 piece root ginger
2 cups rice, wholegrain
3 tbsps (3x15 ml spoons)
  olive oil
4-5 cups chicken stock,
  made with a cube
½ packet frozen peas
pepper
salt

# TURKEY PILAFF**

*For four servings*

1  Wash the rice several times in cold water until the water is clear, then drain.
2  Dice the turkey fillet, the carrots and peppers. Chop the onion. Chop the garlic and ginger finely. Brown the turkey in the olive oil.
3  Remove turkey from pan with a draining spoon. Coat the onion and garlic in the oil. Stir in ginger, carrots and peppers and cook until soft.
4  Add the rice and mix well with the oil and vegetables. Pour in 4 cups of stock, stir in peas, and season with pepper and salt. Simmer for 15 minutes.
5  Return the turkey to the pan. Lower the heat and cover pan with a lid wrapped in a towel.
6  Steam for 15 minutes.

INDIAN RICE WITH TURKEY KEBABS
TURKEY PILAFF

65

# VIETNAMESE RICE WITH TURKEY FILLET**

In Vietnamese cooking, the ingredient which is used most to accompany rice is nuoc mam. This is a light sauce with a fishy aftertaste, which may be prawn-based. Nuoc mam is to the Vietnamese what soy sauce is to the Chinese.

9 oz (250 g) Chinese long-
  grain rice
1 lb 6 oz (600 g) turkey
  fillet
3 large mushrooms
1 pepper
2 tbsps (2x15 ml spoons)
  sesame oil
salt

*For the marinade:*
4 tbsps (4x15 ml spoons)
  soy sauce
2 tbsps (2x15 ml spoons)
  sugar
2 tbsps (2x15 ml spoons)
  dry sherry
1 shallot
1 clove garlic
1 tsp (1x5 ml spoon)
  ground ginger
1 tsp (1x5 ml spoon)
  sesame seeds
nuoc mam

*For four servings*
1   Chop turkey finely.
2   Mix soy sauce with sherry and pinch of salt in a large bowl. Chop the shallot, garlic and ginger finely. Add them to the bowl. Stir sesame seeds into the sauce and season with nuoc mam.
3   Turn the turkey pieces in this marinade. Cover bowl with a sheet of kitchen paper and put into the refrigerator to marinade for several hours.
4   Wash the rice several times until water is clear. Put into a heavy saucepan with a little more than twice its volume of water. Bring to the boil and cook, uncovered, for 15-20 minutes, until all the water has been absorbed.
5   Remove the pan from the heat and cover with a lid wrapped in a towel. Steam for 20 minutes.
6   Cut the mushrooms and peppers into small pieces.
7   Heat the sesame oil in a deep frying pan or a wok. Remove the turkey pieces from the marinade and dry with kitchen paper. Cook the turkey in the oil, stirring continuously.
8   Add the vegetables and cook for 2 more minutes, stirring constantly.
9   Add the marinade and cook for 1 more minute. Serve with the steamed rice.

VIETNAMESE RICE WITH TURKEY FILLET

# RABBIT WITH GINGER AND RICE*

Rabbit is traditionally served with potatoes. If you want to add an exotic touch to this dish, however, why not serve it with rice instead.

2 oz (50 g) fresh ginger
juice of 1 lemon
2¼ lb (1 kg) rabbit, cut
  into pieces
freshly ground pepper
salt
2 tbsps (2x15 ml spoons)
  oil
7 oz (200 g) shallots
3 cloves garlic
1 tbsp (1x15 ml spoon)
  flour
16 fl oz (500 ml) dry
  white wine
bunch parsley, chopped
2 bay leaves
½ stick cinnamon
9 oz (250 g) rice
1 lb 6 oz (600 g) leeks
1 tbsp (1x15 ml spoon)
  butter
9 oz (250 g) tomatoes

*For four servings*

1 Peel the ginger, chop it finely and sprinkle with lemon juice.
2 Season the rabbit pieces with pepper and salt. Fry in oil until well browned. Preheat oven to 225°C/425°F or Gas Mark 7.
3 Peel the shallots, add them to the meat and cook for 3 minutes.
4 Peel the garlic cloves and chop finely. Add garlic and ginger to meat. Sprinkle with flour, wine and the lemon juice used for the ginger, and cook.
5 Add the bay leaves, cinnamon and half the parsley. Cover the pan and cook in the oven for 45 minutes.
6 Cook the rice in just over twice its volume of water. Cover the pan and cook very gently for 20 minutes.
7 Cut leeks into pieces. Brown in hot butter for 5 minutes.
8 Add leeks to the rabbit (after the 45 minutes cooking time) and cook for a further 15 minutes, uncovered.
9 Plunge the tomatoes into boiling water for 10 seconds, peel and divide into eight. Reheat them and sprinkle with parsley just before serving.
10 Place tomatoes on the rice and serve with rabbit.

# RICE WITH MEAT

RABBIT WITH GINGER AND RICE

1 onion
4 tbsps (4x15 ml spoons)
 butter
7 oz (200 g) long-grain
 rice
4½ fl oz (125 ml) stock,
 made with a cube
16 fl oz (500 ml) water
pepper
salt
4 pork chops
9 oz (250 g) apricots
4 oz (100 g) fresh, tender
 spinach

# APRICOT AND SPINACH RICE WITH PORK**

*For four servings*

1   Peel and chop the onion finely. Heat 2 tbsps (2x15 ml spoons) butter and glaze the onion.
2   Add the rice, cook for a few minutes and then pour in the stock.
3   Add the water. Cook the rice for a further 15 minutes.
4   Cook the chops in the rest of the butter and season with pepper and salt.
5   Rinse the apricots in cold water, chop them in half and remove the stones. Cut into crescent-shaped slices.
6   Wash and dry the spinach, and chop finely. Mix the apricots and almost all of the spinach into the rice and cook gently for 3-4 minutes.
7   Serve the chops with rice, garnish with a little chopped spinach and a crescent of apricot.

1 onion
2 tbsps (2x15 ml spoons)
 oil
7 oz (200 g) long-grain
 rice
16 fl oz (500 ml) meat
 stock
1 can Mexican mixed
 vegetables, or 1 packet
 frozen peppers, peas and
 sweetcorn
7 oz (200 g) smoked
 bacon
pepper
salt

# MEXICAN RICE WITH SMOKED BACON*

*For four servings*

1   Peel the onion and chop roughly. Glaze onion in hot oil and add rice. Cook for a few minutes, stirring continuously, then gradually pour in the stock.
2   Simmer for 25 minutes. Meanwhile, cut the bacon into fine strips or dice.
3   Fry the bacon until crisp and mix with the rice.
4   Add the Mexican vegetables or defrosted peppers, peas and sweetcorn. Cook until vegetables are hot.
5   Season with pepper and salt.

MEXICAN RICE WITH SMOKED BACON
APRICOT AND SPINACH RICE WITH PORK

71

10½ oz (300 g) rice
salt
¼ oz (10 g) butter
¼ oz (10 g) flour
milk
pepper
salt
nutmeg
10½ oz (300 g) frozen
  peas
7 oz (200 g) ham (in one
  piece)
small piece Mozzarella
  cheese
1 oz (30 g) butter

# CORONET OF RICE WITH PEAS AND HAM**

*For four servings*

1   Cook the rice in salted water, drain and leave to cool.
2   Make a béchamel sauce with the butter, flour and a little milk. Season with salt, pepper and nutmeg.
3   Heat the defrosted peas gently in the béchamel sauce for 5 minutes.
4   Meanwhile, cut Mozzarella and ham into small pieces. Mix them with the rice and three-quarters of the peas.
5   Grease a ring mould generously with butter and fill with the mixture. Press the rice firmly into the mould.
6   Cook in a preheated oven for 40 minutes at 180°C/350°F or Gas Mark 4.
7   Turn out the rice and fill the centre with the rest of the peas.

7 oz (200 g) frozen peas
salt
4 oz (100 g) Parma ham
10½ oz (300 g) rice,
  cooked and cooled
  (could be left-overs)
2 tbsps (2x15 ml spoons)
  groundnut oil
3 eggs
6 oz (150 g) bean sprouts
2 spring onions, chopped
1 tbsp (1x15 ml spoon)
  toasted sesame seeds

# RICE WITH PARMA HAM**

*For four servings*

1   Blanch peas in lightly salted boiling water for 2 minutes, then drain well.
2   Cut the ham into thin strips. Heat a wok, pour groundnut oil into it and heat until it begins to smoke. Cook the rice, stirring constantly.
3   Add the ham and peas, and cook for a further 5 minutes.
4   Beat the eggs lightly until well mixed and add them to the rice with the bean sprouts. Cook for another 2 minutes and sprinkle with onion and sesame seeds.

CORONET OF RICE WITH PEAS AND HAM
RICE WITH PARMA HAM

1 cup American parboiled rice (long-grain)
7 oz (200 g) pig's liver
14 oz (400 g) mixed minced meat
2 tbsps (2x15 ml spoons) oil
1 pepper
2 onions
3 sticks celery
1 tbsp (1x15 ml spoon) flour
pepper
salt
cayenne pepper
bunch spring onions

# CAJUN RICE WITH MINCED MEAT AND LIVER*

*For four servings*

1 Cook the rice for 20 minutes in 2 cups water. Cut the liver into pieces and cook with minced meat in hot oil.
2 Cut up the pepper, onions and celery. Add them to the meat.
3 Add the flour, brown slightly and add 1 cup water. Cook for 30 minutes and season with pepper, salt and cayenne pepper.
4 Add the rice and garnish with small pieces of spring onion.

1 packet frozen scampi tails, peeled
1 lb 6 oz (600 g) braising steak
2 oz (50 g) butter or margarine
2 tbsps (2x15 ml spoons) flour
2 onions
1 Spanish green chilli
1 stick celery
4 shallots
2 tbsps (2x15 ml spoons) parsley, chopped
9 oz (250 g) fresh mushrooms
1 can peeled tomatoes
16 fl oz (500 ml) beef stock, made from a cube
7 oz (200 g) long-grain rice
pinch cayenne
pepper pinch dried thyme
1 bay leaf
pepper
salt

# BEEF JAMBALAYA**

*For six servings*

1 Defrost the scampi tails and cut the beef into small dice. Cut up the onions, chilli, celery and shallots finely.
2 Brown the meat on all sides in hot butter or margarine. Sprinkle the flour over the meat and mix thoroughly.
3 Add the onions, chilli, celery and shallots, and cook for a few minutes.
4 Add the tomatoes with their juice, together with the mushrooms, thyme, bay leaf and scampi tails.
5 Add the stock, season with pepper, salt and cayenne pepper, and add rice. Make sure the ingredients are covered with stock; if necessary, add more stock.
6 Cover pan, reduce heat and simmer. The rice will be ready after 20-25 minutes. When the meat is tender, season with pepper, salt and cayenne pepper.
7 Serve with a glass of chilled white wine or beer.

CAJUN RICE WITH MINCED MEAT AND LIVER
BEEF JAMBALAYA

2 medium onions
1 clove garlic
1½ oz (40 g) butter
2 oz (50 g) pine kernels or
  flaked almonds
10½ oz (300 g) rice
  (medium or long-grain)
27-35 fl oz (750 ml-1 litre)
  stock, made from a cube
2 oz (50 g) grapes
pepper
salt
½ tsp (0.5x5 ml spoon)
  freshly ground coriander

*Accompany with*
4 lamb chops
pepper
salt
2 lamb's kidneys
2 small aubergines
olive oil for cooking
4 small tomatoes

1 leg of lamb
  (2¼-3½ lb/1-1.5 kg)
4 tbsps (4x15 ml spoons)
  olive oil
3 onions, chopped
3 cloves garlic, chopped
1 carrot, diced
1 lb 2 oz (500 g) tomatoes
sprig of fresh rosemary
sprig of fresh mint
juice of 1 lemon
pepper
salt
9 oz (250 g) long-grain
  rice
2 oz (60 g) grapes
1½ oz (40 g) butter

# ORIENTAL LAMB PILAFF*

*For four servings*

1   Peel and chop the onion and garlic finely.
    Glaze onion and garlic in hot butter. Add
    the pine kernels, rice and stock.
2   Add the grapes and season with pepper, salt
    and coriander. Cook gently for 20 minutes.
3   Slice the aubergines widthways and
    sprinkle the slices with salt.
4   Heat the olive oil in two frying pans. Fry
    the chops and kidneys in one and the
    aubergines in the other.
5   Slice the tomatoes and cook in the
    aubergine oil.
6   Put pilaff on to a dish and arrange the
    aubergine, chops, kidneys and tomatoes
    on top.

# LEG OF LAMB WITH
# RICE PILAFF*

*For 6-8 servings*

1   Heat half the olive oil in a pan. Brown the
    lamb on all sides in the hot oil and then
    remove from pan.
2   Put the vegetables into an oiled pan and
    cover with the remaining oil. Put the
    lamb on top. Season with rosemary, mint,
    pepper and salt.
3   Cook the lamb for 2 hours in a preheated
    oven at 200°C/400°F or Gas Mark 6,
    basting with cooking juices from time to
    time. Pour lemon juice into the pan used
    for browning the lamb. Glaze for 1
    minute then add to oven dish.
4   Meanwhile, put the rice into a saucepan
    containing 16 fl oz (500 ml) water and
    season with pepper and salt. Bring to the
    boil and cook gently for 10 minutes.
5   Stir in grapes and cook for a further 10
    minutes. Add the butter just before
    serving with the lamb.

LEG OF LAMB WITH RICE PILAFF
ORIENTAL LAMB PILAFF

INDIAN LAMB CURRY
LAMB KEBABS WITH APRICOTS

SCHASCHLIK

2¾ lb (1.2kg) shoulder of
    lamb
1 large aubergine (about
    10½ oz/300 g)
24 thin slices smoked
    bacon
24 small onions, peeled
1 orange
5 tbsps (5x15 ml spoons)
    olive oil
6 tbsps (6x15ml spoons)
    dry white wine
freshly ground pepper
1 large onion
2¼ lb (1kg) apricots,
    stoned
fresh mint leaves
2 tbsps (2x15ml spoons)
    liquid honey
2 tbsps (2x15ml spoons)
    brown crystallized sugar
salt
10½ oz (300g) long-grain
    rice

# LAMB KEBABS WITH APRICOTS*

*For six servings*

1 Remove most of the fat from the lamb shoulder and cut the meat into 1½-inch (4 cm) dice.

2 Remove the stalk from the aubergine and cut flesh into 1½- inch (4 cm) dice. Wrap aubergine in bacon slices and secure with cocktail sticks.

3 Grate orange zest into a bowl. Squeeze the orange and add juice to the zest. Add 4 tbsps (4x15 ml spoons) olive oil, 3 tbsps (3x15 ml spoons) wine and pepper.

4 Put the meat, aubergine and onions into a dish, pour on the orange marinade and put into refrigerator to marinate for 2 hours.

5 Peel and chop the large onion finely. Chop half the apricots.

6 Brown the chopped onion for 3 minutes in the rest of the olive oil. Add the chopped apricots, the rest of the wine, the honey and sugar, and cook gently, stirring constantly.

7 Bring the rice to the boil in double its volume of lightly salted water. Cover the pan and reduce the heat. Cook for 20 minutes.

8 Meanwhile, cook the meat on a barbecue or in a preheated oven at 220°C/425°F or Gas Mark 7, or under the grill.

9 Prepare kebabs by alternating pieces of meat, aubergine, onions, mint leaves and apricot halves on skewers.

10 Cook kebabs on a barbecue or grill set about 5 inches (12 cm) from the heat for 10 minutes, turning from time to time.

11 Season with salt and serve with rice and honey and apricot sauce.

1 lb 2 oz (500 g) lamb
  (shoulder, best end of
  neck)
1 large onion
2 cloves garlic
1 apple
1 banana
1 oz (30 g) butter or
  margarine
2 tbsps (2x15 ml spoons)
  curry powder (spicy)
1 tsp (1x5 ml spoon)
  turmeric
cardamom seeds
1 tsp (1x5 ml spoon)
  garam masala (Indian
  mixed spices)
pinch chilli powder
pepper
salt
2 cups basmati rice
2 tbsps (2x15 ml spoons)
  natural yoghurt
bunch chives, chopped

# INDIAN LAMB CURRY**

*For four servings*

1　Cut the lamb into small pieces. Chop the onion and garlic. Peel and core the apple and cut into pieces. Peel and slice the banana.
2　Brown the meat on all sides in hot butter or margarine. Stirring continuously, add curry powder, turmeric and a few cardamom seeds. Cook for a few minutes and then add onion and garlic.
3　Cook for 3 minutes, then pour in water until meat is just covered. Cook gently for 50 minutes.
4　Add banana, apple, chilli, garam masala, pepper and salt to the curry.
5　Wash the rice and put into pan with double its volume of lightly salted water. Cover the pan and cook gently for 15 minutes.
6　After this time, reduce heat of curry and stir yoghurt into the sauce. Check the seasoning.
7　Serve with rice garnished with chopped chives.

1 lb 6 oz (600 g) lamb
7 oz (200 g) smoked
  bacon, in one piece
2 large onions
2 small tomatoes
1 red pepper
1 yellow pepper
1 green pepper
oil
pepper
salt
9 oz (250 g) long-grain
  rice
1 oz (30 g) butter

# SCHASCHLIK*

*For four servings*

1　Cut lamb and bacon into cubes. Clean and cut up pepper. Alternate pieces of meat, bacon, onion, half tomatoes, and pepper on skewers.
2　Season with pepper and salt, and coat with oil.
3　Grill or cook on a rotisserie in an oven at 220°C/425°F or Gas Mark 7 for 20 minutes, turning from time to time.
4　Meanwhile, cook the rice in double its volume of water. Add a knob of butter just before serving.

1 lb 2 oz (500 g) green
 beans
2 kohlrabi
3 tomatoes, diced
1 lb 2 oz (500 g) peas
7 oz (200 g) carrots
1 red pepper
4 tbsps (4x15 ml spoons)
 olive oil
1 tsp (1x5 ml spoon)
 paprika powder
pinch ginger
a few cumin seeds
pepper
salt
a few saffron strands
juice of 1 lemon
2¼ lb (1 kg) lamb (best
 end of neck, stewing)
10½ oz (300 g) long-grain
 rice
1½ oz (40 g) butter

# TUNISIAN LAMB TAJINE WITH RICE**

*For eight servings*

1  Cut the beans, kohlrabi, carrots and pepper into pieces and blanch separately in salted water. Leave to drain.
2  Heat the olive oil in a heavy pan and brown meat on all sides.
3  Season the meat with ginger, saffron, pepper, salt, paprika and cumin. Cover the pan and cook for 45 minutes.
4  Add the diced tomatoes, blanched vegetables and lemon juice. Simmer for 30 minutes.
5  Cook the rice in double its volume of water. Add a knob of butter just before serving.
6  Add the peas to the meat 3 minutes before the end of the cooking time, and serve immediately.

2¼ lb (1 kg) lamb
 (shoulder or leg)
4½ lb (2 kg) turnips
1 tsp (1x5 ml spoon)
 freshly ground black
 pepper
salt
a few saffron strands
1 tsp (1x5 ml spoon)
 paprika powder
4 tbsps (4x15 ml spoons)
 olive oil
1 large onion
2 tomatoes
handful parsley, chopped
10½ oz (300 g) long-grain
 rice
1½ oz (40 g) butter
green olives, stoned

# MOROCCAN LAMB TAJINE WITH RICE**

*For 6-8 servings*

1  Cut the meat into pieces. Peel and quarter the turnips. Blanch the turnip quarters in boiling water for 5 minutes, then drain.
2  Heat the oil in a heavy pan, brown the meat and add the spices.
3  Slice the onions and tomatoes into circles. Cook the turnips for 5 minutes then add to the meat together with the onion and tomatoes.
4  Sprinkle parsley on to vegetables. Cover pan and simmer gently for 20 minutes.
5  Cook the rice as in above recipe and stir in a knob of butter just before serving. Garnish with olives.

MOROCCAN LAMB TAJINE WITH RICE
TUNISIAN LAMB TAJINE WITH RICE

1 lb 6 oz (600 g) stewing
  pork, boned
1 tbsp (1x15 ml spoon)
  margarine
2 small red Spanish chillis
3-4 onions (7 oz/200 g)
4½ fl oz (125 ml) red wine
8 fl oz (250 ml) meat
  stock, made from a cube
4 oz (100 g) bean sprouts
1 pineapple
  (about 2½ lb/1.2 kg)
pepper
salt
3 tsps (3x5 ml spoons)
  paprika powder
pinch chilli powder
9 oz (250 g) long-grain
  rice

# PORK CREOLE WITH RICE**

*For four servings*

1  Chop the meat into cubes and brown a few at time in hot margarine.
2  Remove seeds from the chillis and cut them into thin strips.
3  Peel and chop the onion. Add to the meat and fry.
4  Add the wine and stock and simmer for 40 minutes.
5  Put the rice in a pan with double its volume of water. When boiling, cover the pan and reduce the heat. Steam rice for 20 minutes.
6  Rinse the bean sprouts, add them to the meat and simmer for 10 minutes.
7  Peel the pineapple and remove central core. Slice the fruit, then cut into pieces and add to meat. Heat in the sauce and season with pepper, salt, paprika and chilli powder.

juice of 3 lemons
4 shallots
2 cloves garlic
pepper
salt
1 packet mixed wild rice
8 lamb chops
2 eggs
3 tbsps (3x15 ml spoons)
  milk
3 tbsps (3x15 ml spoons)
  flour
breadcrumbs
2 oz (50 g) butter or
  margarine
parsley

# LAMB CHOPS WITH WILD RICE**

*For four servings*

1  Peel the shallots and garlic. Chop shallots and crush garlic cloves. Mix the lemon juice with the shallots, garlic, pepper and salt.
2  Marinade the lamb chops in lemon juice mixture for 1 hour, then drain and dry with kitchen paper.
3  Meanwhile, cook the wild rice following instructions on the packet.
4  Lightly beat the eggs with the milk. Coat the lamb chops with flour, shaking off any excess, then dip in beaten egg and breadcrumbs.
5  Cook chops gently in margarine or butter for 5 minutes on each side.

LAMB CHOPS WITH WILD RICE
PORK CREOLE WITH RICE

# PORK WITH CHINESE CABBAGE**

Like most Chinese food, this dish is best cooked in a wok.

10½ oz (300 g) Chinese rice
1 oz (25 g) dried Chinese mushrooms
1 lb 6 oz (600 g) lean pork fillet
salt
2 tbsps (2x15 ml spoons) cornflour
bunch spring onions
1 clove garlic
¼ oz (10 g) fresh ginger
1 Chinese cabbage
9 oz (250 g) carrots
2 tbsps (2x15 ml spoons) oil
1 tbsp (1x15 ml spoon) sesame oil
4 tbsps (4x15 ml spoons) soy sauce
3 tbsps (3x15 ml spoons) rice wine (or dry sherry)
1 tbsp (1x15 ml spoon) sugar
1 tbsp (1x15 ml spoon) chilli sauce
4 tbsps (4x15 ml spoons) stock, made from a cube
bunch of chives, chopped

*For six servings*
1 Wash the rice several times until water is clear. Put the rice into a heavy pan with just over double its volume of water. Bring to the boil and cook for 15-20 minutes, uncovered, until all the water has been absorbed.
2 Remove pan from heat and cover with the lid wrapped in a towel. Steam for 20 minutes.
3 Soak Chinese mushrooms in lukewarm water.
4 Chop the meat into cubes, salt lightly and coat cubes in cornflour, shaking off any excess.
5 Cut Chinese cabbage into 1-inch (3 cm) pieces. Cut carrots into thick strips. Slice spring onions thinly. Chop garlic and ginger finely.
6 Heat the oil in a wok or a heavy frying pan and fry meat, a few pieces at a time, for 2 minutes, turning all the time.
7 Remove meat with a draining spoon and brown onions, garlic and ginger in the remaining oil.
8 Add mushrooms, vegetables and sesame oil. Cook briskly for 3 minutes, turning all the time.
9 Return the meat to the pan and add soy sauce, wine, sugar, chilli sauce and the stock.
10 Sprinkle with chives and serve with rice in separate Chinese bowls for each guest.

PORK WITH CHINESE CABBAGE

# CHINESE STEAK WITH RICE*

Cooking in a wok is very quick. All the ingredients should be prepared before you start cooking. They should be cut into pieces or chopped so that they fry quickly when you put them into the oil. The method of cooking in a wok is called stir-frying.

9 oz (250 g) Chinese rice
14 oz (400 g) steak (fillet or tournedo)
1 tbsp (1x15 ml spoon) dry sherry
1 tbsp (1x15 ml spoon) soy sauce
1 tbsp (1x15 ml spoon) maize flour
2 oz (50 g) dried Chinese mushrooms
1 carrot
1 green pepper
1 can bamboo shoots
1 piece fresh root ginger
1 tbsp (1x15 ml spoon) sesame oil
2 tbsps (2x15 ml spoons) oyster sauce
3 tbsps (3x15 ml spoons) stock, made from a cube

*For four servings*

1  Wash the rice several times until the water is clear. Put rice into a heavy pan with just over double its volume of water. Bring to the boil and cook for 15-20 minutes, uncovered, until all the water has been absorbed.

2  Remove the pan from heat and cover with the lid wrapped in a towel. Steam for 20 minutes.

3  Cut the meat into strips and marinate for 10 minutes in a mixture of sherry, soy sauce and flour.

4  Soak the mushrooms in lukewarm water. Cut the pepper and carrot into pieces of equal size.

5  Drain the bamboo shoots, peel the ginger and cut it into thin slices and then into *julienne.*

6  Remove the meat from the marinade with a draining spoon and drain it.

7  Heat a wok or heavy pan, pour in sesame oil and cook meat for 2 minutes, turning all the time.

8  Brown the vegetables for 1 minute in the oil. Add the oyster sauce, stock and meat and cook for 1 minute, turning from time to time.

9  Serve with rice in separate Chinese bowls for each guest.

CHINESE STEAK WITH RICE

# INDONESIAN RICE
# (NASI GORENG)**

The Indonesian spices, ketjap manis and sambal oelek, can be found in Asian shops and some supermarkets.

9 oz (250 g) long-grain
  rice
salt
7 oz (200 g) small white
  onions
oil for frying
7 oz (200 g) pork fillet
  (left-over chops or pork
  can be used)
1 large onion
2 cloves garlic, chopped
1 x 1-inch (2 cm) piece
  fresh ginger
6 oz (150 g) fresh
  mushrooms
1 green pepper
1 red pepper
1 tsp (1x5 ml spoon)
  turmeric
dash of ketjap manis
  (Indonesian soy sauce)
dash of sambal oelek
1 tsp (1x5 ml spoon)
  ground coriander
1 tsp (1x5 ml spoon)
  prawn paste (from Asian
  shops)
4 oz (100 g) bean sprouts
4 oz (100 g) frozen peas
4 tbsps (4x15 ml spoons)
  coconut milk
juice of ½ lemon
2 eggs, beaten
bunch fresh coriander

*For six servings*

1  Cook the rice in plenty of lightly salted water. Rinse the cooked rice in cold water and drain in a sieve.
2  Peel the small onions and slice into circles. Brown the onions in very hot oil until crisp and then drain.
3  Chop the pork fillet into small pieces. Cook them in water with a little salt, then drain.
4  Peel the large onion and garlic cloves. Chop both roughly. Peel the ginger and cut into thin strips.
5  Slice or dice mushrooms and peppers.
6  Heat some oil in a wok or a frying pan until it begins to smoke and brown chopped onion and garlic for 1 minute, turning all the time.
7  Add the ginger, turmeric, ketjap manis, sambal oelek, ground coriander and prawn paste and cook for 3 minutes.
8  Add the meat, mushrooms, bean sprouts, peppers and peas, and cook for 5 minutes, stirring constantly.
9  Add the rice and mix well.
10  Add coconut milk and cook until it begins to evaporate.
11  Cook the eggs in a non-stick frying pan. Leave the omelette to cool and then roll up and cut into thin slices.
12  Pour the nasi goreng into a large dish and garnish with fried onions, strips of omelette and coriander leaves.

INDONESIAN RICE (NASI GORENG)

3½ lb (1.5 kg) beef
3 oz (80 g) margarine
freshly ground pepper
salt
cayenne pepper
4 fl oz (100 ml) passion
   fruit juice
4 fl oz (100 ml) pineapple
   juice, unsweetened
4 oz (100 g) coconut
   cream (canned)
14 oz (400 g) long-grain
   rice
1 large or 2 small
   mangoes
bunch spring onions
grated zest of ½ lime
2 tbsps (2x15 ml spoons)
   lime juice
bunch chives, chopped

# CARIBBEAN BRAISED BEEF WITH RICE*

*For six servings*

1  Cut the meat into small dice and brown on all sides.
2  Season with pepper, salt and cayenne pepper. Add the fruit juices and coconut cream. Cover the pan and simmer for 1½ hours.
3  Put the rice in a pan with double its volume of water. Bring to the boil, then cover, reduce heat and steam for 20 minutes.
4  Peel the mango, remove stone and dice the flesh. Peel and cut the onions into rings. Add mango and onion to meat 10 minutes before the end of the cooking time.
5  Season with lime zest, lime juice, salt and pepper.
6  Sprinkle with chopped chives.

2¼ lb (1 kg) stewing steak
1 large onion
2 cloves garlic
2 firm tomatoes
4-5 tbsps (4-5x15 ml
   spoons) olive oil
2 tbsps (2x15 ml spoons)
   flour
2 bay leaves
½ stick cinnamon
pepper
salt
pinch cumin
4½ fl oz (125 ml) red wine
1 lb 11 oz (750 g) small
   onions
9 oz (250 g) long-grain
   rice
bunch parsley
1-2 tbsps (1-2x15 ml
   spoons) red wine
   vinegar

# GREEK BEEF CASSEROLE WITH RICE*

*For six servings*

1  Cut the meat into dice. Peel the onion and garlic. Chop the onion finely. Chop the tomatoes roughly.
2  Heat the oil in a pan and brown the meat.
3  Stir in the flour, onion, garlic cloves, tomatoes and spices, and cook.
4  Add the wine and enough hot water to cover the ingredients. Simmer for 1 hour.
5  Peel the small onions and add to pan. Add the rice and simmer for another 30 minutes, without stirring.
6  Chop the parsley and mix into the casserole. Season with pepper, salt and vinegar to taste.

CARIBBEAN BRAISED BEEF WITH RICE
GREEK BEEF CASSEROLE WITH RICE

1 lb 6 oz (600 g) braising
  steak
3 cloves garlic, crushed
freshly ground pepper
salt
10½ oz (300 g) ham
  (sliced)
1-3 onions
2 carrots
1 leek
2 sticks celery
4 oz (100 g) mushrooms
3 tbsps (3x15 ml spoons)
  olive oil
1 bouquet garni
  containing orange zest,
  sprig of thyme,
  rosemary and parsley,
  2 bay leaves, 2 cloves
2 tbsps (2x15 ml spoons)
  tomato purée
4½ fl oz (125 ml) dry
  white wine
4½ fl oz (125 ml) water
7 oz (200 g) wild rice

# SPICY STUFATU*

*For four servings*

1   Cut the meat into pieces, season with garlic, salt and pepper and wrap each piece in a slice of ham.
2   Roughly chop the onions, carrots, leek and celery. Chop the mushrooms stalks finely but leave the caps whole.
3   Cook the meat in hot oil, remove from pan and arrange pieces side by side in a casserole.
4   Cook the vegetables and herbs in the oil from the meat. Add tomato purée, wine and water to the vegetables.
5   Cook until the vegetables are soft and then pour on to the meat.
6   Cover the casserole and cook for 1-1½ hours in a preheated oven at 180°C/350°F or Gas Mark 4.
7   Meanwhile, cook the rice for 40 minutes.
8   Remove the bag of herbs from pan and serve the 'stufatu' with wild rice.

1 slice white bread
10 cloves garlic
4 tbsps (4x15 ml spoons)
  olive oil
1¾ lb (800 g) veal
4 tbsps (4x15 ml spoons)
  tomato purée
thyme
marjoram
pepper
salt
2 glasses dry white wine
7 oz (200 g) wild rice

# VEAL WITH GARLIC AND WILD RICE*

*For four servings*

1   Peel the garlic cloves. Cut the veal into small pieces. Brown the pieces of meat on all sides in the olive oil.
2   Crumble the slice of white bread into crumbs.
3   Add breadcrumbs, garlic, tomato purée, thyme, marjoram, pepper, salt and lastly the wine to the meat. Cover the pan and cook for 1 hour.
4   Cook the wild rice for 40-45 minutes and then add to the meat.

SPICY STUFATU
VEAL WITH GARLIC AND WILD RICE

# SAUTÉ VEAL WITH ARTICHOKES AND RICE**

Fresh artichokes are available from greengrocers and supermarkets. If you have trouble finding them, however, you can use tinned artichokes. Meat for sauté veal is cut from the breast, shoulder or spare ribs.

7 tender artichokes
vinegar or lemon juice
9 oz (250 g) long-grain
  rice
1 lb 6 oz (600 g) veal
pinch white pepper
2 tbsps (2x15 ml spoons)
  butter for cooking
salt
4 oz (100 g) fresh
  mushrooms
2 tomatoes
2 shallots
1 tbsp (1x15 ml spoon)
  tomato purée
7 fl oz (200 ml) stock,
  made from a cube
2 tbsps (2x15 ml spoons)
  single cream
1 tbsp (1x15 ml spoon)
  parsley, chopped

*For four servings*
1   Cook the artichokes for 20 minutes in water with a little vinegar or lemon juice. Allow to cool, remove the outside leaves and chokes, and cut the hearts into fairly large pieces.
2   Cook the rice in double its volume of water. Cover the pan and turn off the heat. Steam for 20 minutes without lifting the lid.
3   Season the veal with pepper, and cook for 3 minutes on each side in 1 tbsp (1x15 ml spoon) butter. Cover the pan and simmer for 5 minutes. Remove meat from pan, add salt to taste and keep hot.
4   Plunge the tomatoes into boiling water for 10 seconds, then peel and quarter them and remove the seeds. Chop the flesh finely.
5   Slice the mushrooms. Brown the tomatoes, mushrooms and artichoke pieces for 3-4 minutes in the rest of the butter. Remove from pan and keep hot.
6   Peel and chop the shallots finely. Fry shallots for 2-3 minutes in the cooking juices.
7   Add the tomato purée and stock, and cook briskly for 5 minutes. Add the cream and mix well. Leave to thicken for 2 minutes.
8   Serve the rice with the vegetable mixture and sauté veal. Pour the sauce on top and sprinkle with chopped parsley.

SAUTÉ VEAL WITH ARTICHOKES AND RICE

1 oz (30 g) dried wild
   mushrooms
4 knuckles of veal
pepper
salt
flour
1 stick celery
1 carrot
1 small onion
2 (2x15 ml spoons) olive
   oil
1 oz (25 g) butter
½ glass dry white wine
1 bay leaf
1 can mushrooms
2 tbsps (2x15 ml spoons)
   tomato purée or tomato
   sauce
2 cups stock, made with a
   cube
9 oz (250 g) long-grain
   rice
1 clove garlic
handful parsley
grated lemon rind

# OSSOBUCCO WITH WILD MUSHROOMS AND RICE**

*For four servings*

1  Soak the dried mushrooms in lukewarm water. Sprinkle the veal knuckles with pepper and salt, and coat with flour.

2  Chop the celery and carrot into small pieces. Peel and chop the onion finely. Brown onion in the oil.

3  Add the knuckles of veal and brown on each side. Pour wine over the veal.

4  Remove knuckles from the pan and set aside. Put chopped vegetables and bay leaf into pan, add drained mushrooms, tomato purée and stock. Put the veal knuckles on top.

5  Cook for 1 hour.

6  Cook the rice in double its volume of water. When the water is boiling, reduce heat and simmer for 20 minutes.

7  Chop garlic and parsley finely. Stir garlic, parsley and grated lemon rind into the sauce 10 minutes before the end of the cooking time.

8  Remove bay leaf before serving.

8 thin slices veal
freshly ground pepper
8 thin slices ham
8 fresh sage leaves
9 oz (250 g) long-grain
   rice
16 fl oz (500 ml) chicken
   stock, made from a cube
a few saffron strands
1 oz (30 g) margarine for
   cooking
½ glass white wine
meat extract

# SALTIMBOCCA ALLA ROMANA WITH RICE AND SAFFRON**

*For four servings*

1  Season the veal with salt and pepper. Put a sage leaf and a slice of ham on each piece of veal.

2  Mix saffron with the stock and stir the rice into this mixture. Cook very gently for 15 minutes.

3  Cook slices of veal, ham side up, in a heavy frying pan for 20 minutes or until tender.

4  Add wine to the cooking juice. Reduce and add meat extract.

SALTIMBOCCA ALLA ROMANA WITH RICE AND SAFFRON
OSSOBUCCO WITH WILD MUSHROOMS AND RICE

99

1 lb 2 oz (500 g) onions
2 oz (50 g) butter or
  margarine
1-2 tbsps (1-2x15 ml
  spoons) brown sugar
4½ fl oz (125 ml)
  vegetable stock, made
  from a cube
4 oz (100 g) prunes,
  stoned
9 oz (250 g) long-grain
  rice
4 slices calves' liver
  (1 lb 2 oz/500 g)
1 oz (30 g) flour
2 tbsps (2x15 ml spoons)
  oil
2 tbsps (2x15 ml spoons)
  cider vinegar
salt
freshly ground pepper

# CALVES' LIVER WITH ONIONS AND PRUNES**

*For four servings*

1  Put rice into double its volume of water and bring to the boil. Cover and turn off heat. Steam for 20 minutes.
2  Cut the onions in half and then into rings. Brown onions in 1 oz (30 g) butter or margarine and sprinkle with brown sugar. Add stock and cook gently for 5 minutes.
3  Cut the prunes into strips, add to the pan and simmer for 5 minutes.
4  Coat the liver in flour. Heat the rest of the butter or margarine. Add liver and cook gently for 2 minutes on each side.
5  Season onion mixture with cider vinegar, pepper and salt, pour on to veal and serve with rice.

4 medium slices calves'
  liver
bunch leeks
1 piece ginger
  (½ inch/1 cm)
9 oz (250 g) long-grain
  rice
3 oz (70 g) butter
1 tbsp (1x15 ml spoon)
  vinegar
pepper
salt
sprig of thyme
grated zest of ¼ lemon
1 tsp (1x5 ml spoon)
  cornflour
2 tbsps (2x15 ml spoons)
  parsley, chopped

# CALVES' LIVER WITH LEEKS*

*For four servings*

1  Cut slices of liver into ½ inch (1 cm) strips. Remove green part of leeks and cut white parts into 2½ inch (6 cm) pieces. Peel the ginger and slice finely.
2  Cook the rice in double its volume of water for 20 minutes.
3  Melt half the butter in a frying pan, brown the leeks and add vinegar and a glass of water. Season with salt and pepper, and add sprig of thyme.
4  Fry liver quickly in the rest of the butter, add ginger, and season with salt and pepper.
5  Sprinkle liver with grated lemon zest.
6  Thicken the cooking juice with cornflour and stir in parsley.

CALVES' LIVER WITH LEEKS
CALVES' LIVER WITH ONIONS AND PRUNES

# FLEMISH RICE WITH BROWN SUGAR*

This is a very old traditional Flemish dish. The use of saffron is probably a result of Spanish influence.

2½ pints (1.5 litres) milk
zest of 1 lemon
7 oz (200 g) dessert rice
a few saffron strands
dark brown sugar

*For 4-6 servings*

1  Bring milk to the boil with a little lemon zest and add the washed rice.
2  Cook rice gently for 1 hour, stirring from time to time.
3  Add the saffron strands a few minutes before the end of the cooking time.
4  Pour the hot rice into dessert plates and leave to set and cool.
5  Serve with brown sugar.

# BAVARIAN RICE*

2 oz (50 g) grapes
1 liqueur glass rum
16 fl oz (500 ml) milk
pinch salt
4 oz (100 g) dessert rice
3 leaves gelatine
6 oz (150 g) sugar
2 drops vanilla essence
2 tsps (2x5 ml spoons) instant coffee
7 oz (200 g) whipping cream

*For 4-6 servings*

1  Soak the grapes in rum.
2  Bring milk to the boil with salt and cook rice in it until all the milk has been absorbed.
3  Remove from heat and add the grapes.
4  Soak the gelatine in cold water, cut into pieces and dissolve in hot rice.
5  Stir in sugar, vanilla essence and coffee. Leave to cool.
6  Whip the cream and stir into rice. Rinse a pudding mould in cold water and pour mixture in.
7  Bang mould against a worktop so that the rice settles evenly. Put into the refrigerator for 1½ hours to set.
8  Just before serving, plunge the mould into hot water and turn out the pudding on to a serving dish.

# RICE DESSERTS

BAVARIAN RICE
FLEMISH RICE WITH BROWN SUGAR

EMPRESS RICE
RICE TART WITH RASPBERRY JELLY

RICE AND APRICOT MOULD

6 oz (150 g) dried apricots
1 glass sweet white wine
9 oz (250 g) dessert rice
28 fl oz (800 ml) milk
1 piece lemon zest
4¼ oz (115 g) caster sugar
8 fl oz (250 ml) whipping
  cream
2 egg whites
redcurrants

# RICE AND APRICOT MOULD**

*For six servings*

1 Soak the apricots in wine and then cook. Leave to cool.
2 Wash rice and bring to the boil in 1¾ pints (1 litre) lightly salted water. Cook for 8 minutes on medium heat.
3 Drain rice in a sieve. Boil the milk with the lemon zest, add the rice and cook gently for 45 minutes, stirring from time to time.
4 Remove from heat, add 3½ oz (80 g) sugar and a pinch of salt. Pour into a large bowl, cover and leave to cool.
5 Whip the cream until firm and add 1 oz (30 g) sugar.
6 Beat egg whites until stiff. Fold cream and then egg whites into the rice.
7 Set aside 2 apricots, cut into strips. Alternate layers of rice and apricots in a pudding mould. Put into the refrigerator until the rice has set firm.
8 Turn out on to a serving dish and decorate with redcurrants and strips of apricot.

3 fl oz (70 ml) milk
7 oz (200 g) dessert rice
pinch cinnamon
4 oz (100 g) softened
  butter
3 eggs, separated
1 oz (30 g) sugar
raspberry juice
3 leaves gelatine
fresh raspberries for
  garnish
sprig of fresh mint

# RICE TART WITH RASPBERRY JELLY**

*For four servings*

1 Bring milk and rice to the boil and add cinnamon. Simmer until all the milk has been absorbed and the rice is cooked, then allow to cool.
2 Beat the egg yolks with butter and sugar, and add rice.
3 Beat the egg whites until stiff and fold gently into rice.
4 Pour rice into a round tart tin and stand in a 'bain-Marie'. Cook for 1 hour in a preheated oven at 175°C/350°F or Gas Mark 4.

5 Turn tart out into a dish and allow to cool.
6 Soak gelatine in cold water, cut up the leaves and melt in a small pan with the raspberry juice.
7 Slide a large cake ring around the tart. Pour raspberry juice on to tart. Put into the refrigerator to harden.
8 When raspberry topping has set, remove cake ring and decorate with raspberries and mint.

4½ oz (120 g) crystallized fruit
2 tbsps (2x15 ml spoons) white rum
4 oz (100 g) dessert rice
4½ oz (120 g) caster sugar
4 fl oz (100 ml) whipping cream
27 fl oz (750 ml) milk
3 egg yolks
2 leaves gelatine
raspberry juice
1 vanilla pod

# EMPRESS RICE***

*For four servings*

1 Soak the crystallized fruit in rum.
2 Wash the rice and bring to the boil in 1¾ pints (1 litre) water. Cook gently for 8 minutes and drain.
3 Boil 16 fl oz (500 ml) milk, stir rice into milk and cook for 30 minutes, until all the liquid has been absorbed.
4 Remove the rice from heat and stir in 2 oz (60 g) sugar. Allow to cool.
5 Beat the egg yolks with the rest of the sugar until they are white.
6 Boil the rest of the milk with the vanilla pod. Remove the pod and pour the milk on to the egg mixture.
7 Pour the mixture into a pan and thicken without boiling.
8 Soak the gelatine in cold water. Cut into pieces and add to the cream mixture.
9 When the rice and the cream mixture have cooled completely, mix them with the crystallized fruit.
10 Whip chilled cream until firm and fold into the rice.
11 Pour the rice into a pudding mould. Put into refrigerator to set. Serve well chilled with raspberry juice.

16 fl oz (500 ml) milk
1 vanilla pod
1 piece lemon zest
3 oz (75 g) sugar
pinch salt
1 oz (25 g) butter
6 oz (150 g) dessert rice
3 egg yolks
1 egg
breadcrumbs
oil for frying

*For the zabaglione*
4½ oz (125 g) caster sugar
3 egg yolks
4 fl oz (100 ml) dry white
    wine
2 tbsps (2x15 ml spoons)
    white rum
fresh raspberries for
    garnish

# RICE CROQUETTES WITH ZABAGLIONE***

*For four servings*

1  Wash the rice and cook for 1 minute in 16 fl oz (500 ml) water. Drain.
2  Boil milk with scraped vanilla pod, lemon zest, sugar, salt and butter.
3  Mix the rice with boiling milk and turn off heat as soon as milk boils again. Remove the vanilla pod.
4  Steam for 25 minutes.
5  Allow milk to cool a little and then add 3 egg yolks. Allow to cool completely and shape the rice into small balls.
6  Beat the other 3 egg yolks with the sugar until the mixture turns white. Add wine and rum and continue to beat until foamy.
7  Dip the rice balls into beaten single egg and then into breadcrumbs and fry in hot oil.
8  Drain and decorate with fresh raspberries.

1¾ pints (1 litre) milk
1 vanilla pod
1 piece lemon zest
6 oz (150 g) sugar
pinch salt
2 oz (50 g) butter
10½ oz (300 g) dessert rice
6 egg yolks
1 lb 2 oz (500 g)
    strawberries
1 liqueur glass kirsch
raspberry juice
fresh mint leaves

# CORONET OF RICE WITH STRAWBERRIES*

*For six servings*

1  Wash the rice and cook for 1 minute in 1¾ pints (1 litre) water. Drain.
2  Bring milk to the boil with scraped vanilla pod, lemon zest, sugar, salt and knob of butter.
3  Mix the rice with boiling milk, cover and turn off the heat when milk boils again. Remove vanilla pod. Cover and steam for 30 minutes.
4  Leave to cool a little, add egg yolks and mix thoroughly.
5  Pour rice mixture into a ring mould and then chill in the refrigerator.
6  Turn out chilled rice and fill the centre with strawberries soaked in kirsch.
7  Pour the raspberry juice over the rice and decorate with mint leaves.

CORONET OF RICE WITH STRAWBERRIES
RICE CROQUETTES WITH ZABAGLIONE

1¾ pints (1 litre) milk
1 vanilla pod
pinch salt
6 oz (150 g) dessert rice
12 oz (350 g) caster sugar
1 heaped dessert spoon
  custard powder
3 egg whites

# SNOW RICE PUDDING**

*For four servings*

1 Bring milk to the boil with scraped
  vanilla pod and salt.
2 Wash the rice and mix it into the boiling
  milk. Cook gently for 30 minutes.
3 Add 6 oz (150 g) sugar and remove
  vanilla pod.
4 Cream custard powder in a little cold
  milk and stir into the rice.
5 Cook for 1 minute and then pour rice into
  an ovenproof dish.
6 Beat egg whites until stiff and add 6 oz
  (150 g) sugar. Spoon the egg white on to
  the rice.
7 Sprinkle with the rest of the sugar and
  cook for 15 minutes in a preheated oven
  at 180°C/350°F or Gas Mark 4.

*For the filling:*
1¾ pints (1 litre) milk
1 vanilla pod
6 oz (150 g) dessert rice
6 oz (150 g) sugar
3 eggs
butter to grease tins

*For the crust:*
10½ oz (300 g) self-raising
  flour
½ oz (15 g) sugar
pinch salt
1 egg
milk
4½ oz (125 g) butter
caster sugar

# RICE TART**

*For two tarts 8 inches (20 cm) in diameter*

1 Bring milk to the boil with vanilla pod.
2 Wash and drain the rice and stir into the
  boiling milk. Cover and simmer for
  1 hour, stirring from time to time.
3 Add the sugar and allow rice to cool.
4 Stir in 3 eggs. Mix well.
5 Pour the flour into a mixing bowl and
  make a well in the middle. Pour sugar into
  the well, add egg, salt and a little milk.
6 Mix well, then work in the butter and
  knead to a smooth dough.
7 Make two balls of dough. When rolled
  out, their diameter should be a little over
  8 inches (20 cm).
8 Butter two 8-inch (20 cm) tart tins and
  line with pastry.
9 Fill pastry casings with the rice mixture
  and cook for 20 minutes in a preheated
  oven at 220°C/425°F or Gas Mark 7.
10 Sprinkle with caster sugar.

SNOW RICE PUDDING
RICE TART

# RICE FRITTERS**

To make this delicious dessert into a real feast, serve the rice fritters with a fruit juice such as raspberry, strawberry or blackberry juice. To give the fritters a different flavour, you can use lager instead of mineral water.

handful grapes
1 liqueur glass rum
6 oz (150 g) dessert rice
16 fl oz (500 ml) milk
3 oz (75 g) caster sugar
4 egg yolks
7 oz (200 g) flour
5 fl oz (150 ml) mineral water
1½ oz (40 g) butter
3 egg whites
oil for frying
caster sugar
salt
1 stick cinnamon

*For 4-6 servings*

1 Soak the grapes in rum.
2 Wash the rice and blanch for 8 minutes in lightly salted water. Drain in a sieve.
3 Bring milk to the boil with the stick of cinnamon. Stir in the rice and bring back to the boil.
4 Cover the pan and simmer for about 30 minutes until all the milk has been absorbed.
5 Remove the pan from the heat and add 2 egg yolks, caster sugar, rum and grapes.
6 Pour the mixture into a dish, cover and put in the refrigerator overnight.
7 Stir the 2 remaining egg yolks and a pinch of salt into the flour.
8 Gradually add the mineral water until you have a thick batter.
9 Melt the butter and add to the batter.
10 Cover and leave to stand for 2 hours in a warm place.
11 Beat the egg whites until stiff and fold gently into batter.
12 Shape the rice into small balls and dip each one into the batter. Fry the fritters, no more than 5 at a time, in hot oil.
13 Drain fritters on kitchen paper.
14 Sprinkle with caster sugar just before serving.

RICE FRITTERS

# INDEX

## SOUPS AND STARTERS

Fish soup with rice ............................................. 18
Genoese risotto ..... ............................................ 22
Mussel soup ...................................................... 18
Pumpkin soup with rice ...................................... 16
Rice croquettes with scampi tails ........................ 26
Rice soufflé ...................................................... 24
Rice tartlets with baked eggs ............................. 24
Risi-bisi .......................................................... 23
Risotto with saffron and peas ............................ 22
Risotto with wild mushrooms and courgettes ........ 23
Spring soup ...................................................... 16
Tomatoes stuffed with rice ................................ 26

## RICE SALADS

Exotic rice salad .............................................. 32
Italian rice salad .............................................. 32
Rice salad with herrings and apple ...................... 30
Rice salad with peppers and artichoke hearts ........ 28
Rice salad with vegetables ................................. 28
Wholegrain rice salad ....................................... 30

## RICE WITH FISH AND SHELLFISH

Black risotto .................................................... 38
Greek pilaff with mussels .................................. 44
Gumbo with prawns .......................................... 36
Jambalaya ....................................................... 34
Japanese sushi rice ........................................... 42
Paella Valenciana ............................................. 40
Risotto with calamari and beans ......................... 38
Turkish pilaff with scampi ................................. 44

## RICE WITH POULTRY

Balkan guinea fowl with rice ............................. 62
Chicken curry .................................................. 54

Chicken livers with glazed leeks ..................................... 53
Exotic rice with chicken ............................................ 46
Indian rice with chicken curry ..................................... 54
Indian rice with turkey kebabs ..................................... 64
Iranian pilaff with chicken ........................................ 58
Rice with breast of duck and ginger ............................... 60
Rice with chicken and lime ........................................ 52
Rice with chicken in sauce diable ................................. 56
Rice with chicken legs and aubergines ............................. 48
Spit-roasted chicken with rice and vegetables ..................... 48
Turkey pilaff ..................................................... 64
Vietnamese rice and turkey fillet ................................. 66

# RICE WITH MEAT

Apricot and spinach rice with pork ................................ 70
Beef jambalaya .................................................... 74
Cajun rice with minced meat and liver ............................. 74
Calves' liver with leeks .......................................... 100
Calves' liver with onions and prunes .............................. 100
Caribbean braised beef with rice .................................. 92
Chinese steak with rice ........................................... 88
Coronet of rice with peas and ham ................................. 72
Greek beef casserole with rice .................................... 92
Indian lamb curry ................................................. 81
Indonesian rice (Nasi Goreng) ..................................... 90
Lamb chops with wild rice ......................................... 84
Lamb kebabs with apricots ......................................... 80
Leg of lamb with rice pilaff ...................................... 76
Mexican rice with smoked bacon .................................... 70
Moroccan lamb tajine with rice .................................... 82
Oriental lamb pilaff .............................................. 76
Ossobucco with wild mushrooms and rice ............................ 98
Pork Creole with rice ............................................. 84
Pork with Chinese cabbage ......................................... 86
Rabbit with ginger and rice ....................................... 68
Rice with Parma ham ............................................... 72
Saltimbocca alla Romana with rice and saffron. ....................98
Sauté veal with artichokes and rice ............................... 96
Schaschlik ........................................................ 81
Spicy stufatu ..................................................... 94
Tunisian lamb tajine with rice .................................... 82
Veal with garlic and wild rice .................................... 94

# RICE DESSERTS

Bavarian rice ..................................................... 102
Coronet of rice with strawberries .................... 108
Empress rice ..................................................... 107
Flemish rice with brown sugar ...................... 102
Rice and apricot mould ................................... 106
Rice croquettes with zabaglione .................... 108
Rice fritters ..................................................... 112
Rice tart ........................................................... 110
Rice tart with raspberry jelly ........................ 106
Snow rice pudding ........................................... 110